The Gothic World of Stephen King

The Gothic World of ~~Stephen King~~ Landscape of Nightmares

Edited by
Gary Hoppenstand and
Ray B. Browne

Bowling Green State University Popular Press
Bowling Green, Ohio 43403

Contents

Introduction:
  The Horror of It All: Stephen King and the
  Landscape of the American Nightmare   1
    Gary Hoppenstand and Ray B. Browne
Blood, Eroticism, and the Vampire in
  Twentieth-Century Popular Literature   20
    Carol A. Senf
Of Mad Dogs and Firestarters—
  The Incomparable Stephen King   31
    Garyn G. Roberts
Reading Between the Lines:
  Stephen King and Allegory   37
    Bernard J. Gallagher
A Blind Date with Disaster: Adolescent Revolt
  in the Fiction of Stephen King   49
    Tom Newhouse
Freaks: The Grotesque as Metaphor in the
  Works of Stephen King   56
    Vernon Hyles
Viewing "The Body":
  King's Portrait of the Artist as Survivor   64
    Leonard G. Heldreth
Stephen King's Creation of Horror in *'Salem's Lot*:
  A Prolegomenon Towards a New Hermeneutic
  of the Gothic Novel   75
    James E. Hicks
Love and Death in the American Car:
  Stephen King's Auto-Erotic Horror   84
    Linda C. Badley
The Dark Tower:
  Stephen King's Gothic Western   95
    James Egan
Taking Stephen King Seriously:
  Reflections on a Decade of Best-Sellers   107
    Samuel Schuman

A Dream of New Life: Stephen King's *Pet Sematary*
  as a Variant of *Frankenstein*   115
    Mary Ferguson Pharr
Stephen King's *Pet Sematary:*
  Hawthorne's Woods Revisited   126
    Tony Magistrale
"Oz the Gweat and Tewwible" and "The Other Side":
  The Theme of Death in *Pet Sematary* and
  Jitterbug Perfume   135
    Natalie Schroeder
Contributors   142

The Horror of It All:
Stephen King and the Landscape
of the American Nightmare

Gary Hoppenstand and Ray B. Browne

"...by becoming a writer of them himself, he had condemned himself to a life of dissection."

Misery, Stephen King

Over the past decade or so, Stephen King has beaten the odds.

He has beaten the publishing odds. Though his first published novel, *Carrie* (1974), was a moderate hardcover success, bringing the author a $2500 advance, it was phenomenally successful as a paperback, garnering a $400,000 bid for the author's paperback rights from New American Library.[1] King's spectacular entry into the mass market arena was even more spectacular when considering the paperback audience of the time: well-educated middle-class women, and the predominate taste of that audience: sex/money/power thrillers and romances.[2] Horror fiction then produced the occasional best-seller, such as Ira Levin's *Rosemary's Baby* (1967) and William Peter Blatty's *The Exorcist* (1971), but for the most part the late 60s and the 70s were the eras of bedroom/corporate gymnastics and pseudo-gothic/historical soft-core erotica, not the eras of Dracula, Frankenstein and the Wolfman. King helped to change that. Today, horror fiction has carved its own predominate niche on the supermarket paperback shelf out of the bloody remains of Harold Robbins and Barbara Cartland and Irving Wallace and Janet Dailey, and the new mass market moguls: Robert McCammon, Charles L. Grant, Clive Barker and Peter Straub, walk in close step up the bestseller list with King. Even the hardcover bastions have fallen to this man. One of his most recent hardcover novels, *It* (1986), had a first printing of 800,000 copies, followed by five additional printings for a total of 1,025,000 hardcover copies published.[3]

1

King also has beaten the writing odds. At a loss to explain his accomplishments as a literary sensation, a number of critics have closely examined his fiction and not liked what they've seen. Some attack his ideas, claiming that the content of his horror fiction is trite and unoriginal: *'Salem's Lot* (1975) is a vampire story and vampire stories have been done to death; *The Shining* (1977) is a mere haunted house tale; or *The Stand* (1978) is simply another end-of-the-world fantasy, and who needs one of *those*? Other critics attack his style, claiming that he has none. In a recent *Time* magazine feature article on King, several of his stylistic nuances were outlined: "The Disgusting Colloquialism," "The Brand-Name Maneuver," "The Comic Strip Effect," "The Burlesque Locution," and "The Fancy Juxtaposition."[4] Of course, if original ideas and writing style are valid measures of success, then William Faulkner and Henry James should be on top of the *New York Times*' bestseller list instead of King.

No, there is something, a *big* something, about the talent of Stephen King that explains why he has beaten such fantastic odds, something that unravels the mystery of why such a critically unpopular author working in such a critically unpopular genre could be such a dominating force in publishing (or in other media, like film, television, audio tapes and comics for that matter). That something might be termed storytelling ability. Perhaps a better descriptive tag would be the "dazzle effect," or the ability to take the reader outside of himself with fiction, to become intimately involved with fiction, to become oblivious to such things as style (or the written word) in a desire to be swept away by the author's vision, to become oblivious to page turning. In other words, the dazzle effect is entertainment, and King has that quality in spades. There are some rather specific elements comprising the King dazzle effect, and this introduction shall examine several of the more prominent facets of this talent.

Let's begin with the author's background. King's rise in popularity as the chronicler of America's nightmares (and the American Nightmare) was sudden, dramatic—though not achieved without a great deal of hard work—and reads like a modern-day Horatio Alger story. He was born September 21, 1947 in Portland, Maine, the second son of Donald and Nellie Ruth (Pillsbury) King. He spent much of his childhood in Fort Wayne, Indiana with his mother (after the separation of his parents in 1949).[5] In a recent interview, King discusses this part of his life:

Inside, I felt different and unhappy a lot of times. I felt *violent* a lot of times. But not a whole lot of that came out, because in the family I came from, there was a high premium on keeping yourself to yourself—on maintaining a pleasant exterior—saying 'please' and 'thank you' and using your handkerchief even if you're on the Titanic and it's going down, because that's the way you were supposed to behave.

But I hung out with the kids. I worked on cars, played sports as much as I could. I was a tuition kid, and it was a long way back and forth, so I wasn't involved in basketball and stuff like that. I had to play football, because I was big. If you didn't play football and you were big, it meant you were a fucking faggot, right? That's what it's like when you come from a small town.

So I kept that other part of myself to myself. I never wanted to let anyone get at it. I figured that they'd steal it, if they knew what I thought about this or that or the other thing. It wasn't the same as being embarrassed about it, so much as wanting to keep it and sort of work it out myself.[6]

The first block of the King myth was firmly in place. Indeed, his life fits that mythic pattern of *The Author*: beginning with the sensitive, misunderstood childhood desiring to express itself in writing. The second block of *The Author* myth was laid when, after uncovering an old box full of 1940s paperbacks (containing an H.P. Lovecraft collection and an Avon sampler), King began, in 1959-60, to write tales of imagination for professional submission,[7] and thus discovered an emotional outlet for personal expression.

From his first professional sale ("The Glass Floor," *Startling Mystery Stories*) in 1967 to the publication of *Carrie*, King sharpened his storytelling skills by writing horror short stories for "men's magazines" like *Cavalier*, and several novels that never found their way to publication.[8] It was a time, according to King, of physical and emotional stress, of a struggle to make it in the writing business. King remembers:

That was not a good year [the winter of his first year of teaching]. I was drinking too much and Tabby [King's wife, Tabitha Jane Spruce, married on January 2, 1971] was not very happy about that. The money I was making as a teacher was not enough to cover our bills; I was selling a few short stories, most to *Cavalier* magazine, but they were not enough to pay the phone bill and we finally asked Ma Bell to come and take the telephone out of our trailer, which sat on a lovely, snow-swept hill in Hermon, Maine. If anyone should ever ask you, Hermon, Maine is not Paris, France. It is not even Twin Forks, Idaho. If it is not the pits, it is very close. Having the phone taken out was our one pitiful act of defiance that year. It was quitting before the Credit Department fired us.

Tabby juggled the bills with the competent but scary expertise of a circus clown juggling tennis racquets; the transmission on our senile 1965 Buick Special began to whine, then to groan, then to chug and hitch; and as the winter came in, the snow-mobiles began to buzz across the fields.[9]

Thus the final block of *The Author* myth, the King myth, the artist at odds with life, was deposited, and this was perhaps the most important factor of the author's life in establishing a reason for the development of the King cult in recent years.

Other horror fiction author cults have evolved in the past: such as with E.A. Poe, Ambrose Bierce, H.P. Lovecraft, and King effectively fits the pattern. An author cult is defined as a group of devoted readers (indeed, almost fanatically obsessive readers) who think the author's life is as important, or more important, than his work. A personality cult generally surrounds a genre author when that author's life tenders unusual experiences, which hence place him or her outside of the mainstream. The personality (or author) cult attaches itself to the author's strangeness or difference, and the author's life is elevated to mythic proportions. The physical products of the author's labor, his books and manuscripts, become icons of worship and hence become of immense money value, inflated far beyond a reasonable worth by the slavish drive of the cult follower to purchase, at any cost, those books and manuscripts. For example, King scholar Douglas Winter states that a first edition hardcover of *Carrie* now sells for $400; a first hardcover of *'Salem's Lot* (in original dust jacket) sells for $500; and first edition hardcovers of *Night Shift* and *Danse Macabre* respectively sell for $200 and $100.[10] And these prices are for mass market editions barely a decade old! In fact, a small press industry has blossomed around the King cult. Book editions of either mass market hardcovers (e.g. *Firestarter, Christine* and *Skeleton Crew*) or unique anthologies (e.g. *The Dark Tower: The Gunslinger*) are printed in artificially small press runs (so-called "limited editions") for the express purpose of making a fantastic profit on vastly inflated prices. And the irony of it all is that often the same exact text is sold at the bookstore for a small fraction of the limited edition price. Even King is a bit perplexed by his cult following. He once wrote a message to Winter inside a first edition of *The Shining* that reads: " 'Here's a True Fact collectors don't seem to know—it's the same story even if you print it on shopping bags...' "[11] Though King is not exceptional because of his cult following, it is unprecedented that his following has grown so quickly. And what really makes King exceptional here is that he functions *both* as a mass market, bestselling author (in the tradition of a Robbins or a Michener) and as a cult author (like a Lovecraft or a Robert E. Howard).

As bestselling fiction, King's work seems to grow in popularity with each new release. Since *Carrie, 'Salem's Lot, The Shining* and *The Stand*, King has published the novels: *The Dead Zone* (1979), *Firestarter* (1980), *Cujo* (1981), *The Dark Tower: The Gunslinger* (1982), *Christine* (1983), *Pet Sematary* (1983), *The Talisman*—with Peter Straub—(1984), *It* (1986), *The Eyes of the Dragon* (1987), *The Dark TowerII*: The Drawing of the Three (1987) and *Misery* (1987). Under the pseudonym "Richard Bachman," King has published the novels *Rage* (1977), *The Long Walk* (1979), *Roadwork* (1981), *The Running Man* (1982) and *Thinner* (1984).

His collections include: *Night Shift* (1978), *Different Seasons* (1982) and *Skeleton Crew* (1985); and along with his four film screen plays: *Creepshow* (1982) *Cat's Eye* (1985), *Silver Bullet* (1985) and *Maximum Overdrive* (1986), he has published a nonfiction study of the horror genre in the mass media, *Danse Macabre* (1981), an art edition novella, *Cycle of the Werewolf (Silver Bullet)* (1983) and a comic book adaptation, *Creepshow* (1982), based on his film of the same name. According to Winter:

> More than fifty million copies of King's books have seen print worldwide, and nearly twenty film projects have been spawned from his writing, while his readers, seemingly insatiable, clamor for more...and more. Beginning in September, 1986, four new King novels will be published in a fourteen-month period, a publishing landmark equivalent to the Beatles holding the top five singles on the *Billboard* charts in January, 1965. One of these novels, *Misery*, is a searing commentary on the price of a writer's fame.[12]

If King's production over the past decade seems fantastic, it's because it is. He works each day at his word processor from 9 a.m. to 5 p.m.—except his birthday, Christmas and the Fourth of July—and he writes about ten pages a day.[13] Thus, King's commercial success is based on two things: first, that he works hard at a consistent, day after day pace (which indeed places him within an Algerian work ethic context), and second, that he possesses an intimate understanding of what his audience desires of his work. He plays *The Author* myth for his cult following, for even though he protests at times about this type of devoted reader, he does nothing to change the *status quo*. He maintains a close relationship with small press publishers, like Donald Grant Books (the publisher of his *The Dark Tower* series); he assists in the production of a fan newsletter, *Castle Rock*; and he has granted more interviews than most other popular novelists. It's as if he fears severing the lines of communication with *The Following* since *The Following* tells him what they want from him, what it takes to produce a bestseller.

What it takes to produce a *horror novel* bestseller, King has figured, is to not change the fundamental motifs of the horror story (those easily recognizable elements like the haunted house or the vampire) but to adapt them to the emotional needs of his audience. One of the reasons why King has become so much more commercially successful than some of his horror writing peers, like Robert Bloch or Richard Matheson (authors who, by King's own admission, are better writers) is because he directs his work at the foundation of the paperback mass market: women and adolescents. Granted, male readers comprise a significant portion of his readership, but King (unlike Bloch, Matheson and other horror genre authors) communicates to those people who normally would *never* pick up a horror novel. Women readers discover in King social melodrama as the significant focus of his fiction, while adolescents recognize in King young protagonists who experience life's problems much the same way as they do.

For example, in *The Shining*, the supernatural motif of the novel is the haunted hotel, but the actual *horror* elements of the story center more with the disintegration of the Torrance family. The Overlook Hotel, despite the supernatural fireworks King throws in there from time to time, is but merely the vehicle that outlines the frightful consequences of a domestic relationship gone dreadfully wrong. *The Shining* is a soap opera that also just happens to be a haunted house novel. Even in King's earlier effort, *'Salem's Lot*, where so much critical attention has been addressed to the fact that it is an update of the traditional vampire story, the manner in which King juxtaposes vampires with the the steamy, sordid New England setting reads like "Dracula comes to Peyton Place." Often, King frames the forthcoming supernatural plot with a domestic sub-plot. In "Children of the Corn," one of the more frightening short stories in the *Night Shift* collection, the story opens with husband and wife, Burt and Vicky Robeson, driving their T-Bird down an isolated Nebraska road. Conflict and tension are quickly established for the reader by their near-murderous relationship:

> Vicky was fanning herself with her scarf even though the T-Bird was air conditioned. 'Where are we, anyway?'
>
> 'Nebraska.'
>
> She gave him a cold, neutral look. 'Yes, Burt. I know we're in Nebraska, Burt. But where the hell *are* we?'
>
> 'You've got the road atlas. Look it up. Or can't you read?'
>
> 'Such wit. This is why we got off the turnpike. So we could look at three hundred miles of corn. And enjoy the wit and wisdom of Burt Robeson.'
>
> He was gripping the steering wheel so hard his knuckles were white. He decided he was holding it that tightly because if he loosened up, why, one of those hands might just fly off and hit the ex-Prom Queen beside him right in the chops. We're saving our marriage, he told himself. Yes. We're doing it the same way us grunts went about saving villages in the war.[14]

Burt's and Vicky's terrible adventures in Gatlin, Nebraska are but a supernaturally magnified augmentation of their own terrible life together. And when they lose their physical direction in that Nebraskan cornfield vacuum, King is telling us that the genuine loss here is with the emotional bankruptcy of the contemporary American marriage. Since the mass appeal of social melodrama for an audience, in particular for a female paperback buying audience, is the formulaic expression of social concerns, naturally marriage (or the destruction of marriage) figures preponderantly in this expression. Many romance formulas detail the successful outcome of a male/female relationship (usually in marriage). King has nicely shown his audience in much of his work the darker side of romance and marriage, and this has found satisfaction with his readers.

As anyone with children who has gone through a painful divorce might tell you, the victims of the divorce are not the husband and wife, but the children. The children in "Children of the Corn" assume a monstrous revenge of their parents' sins by killing them: perhaps the consequence of a bad marriage is bad kids. But the victimized child protagonist is featured throughout King's fiction, and this provides a major attraction for the adolescent and young adult book buyer. Today's younger generation, weaned on video excess (television, video games, video tapes, MTV), rarely delves into the printed page except to survey the latest issue of *Teen Beat* magazine or to complete the dreaded book report homework assignment. King's work here presents an anomaly. The teenager loves to read King. His novels are parked alongside sticker-ridden notebooks on high school students' desks. Dogeared copies of *Carrie, The Shining* and *The Stand* are crammed into lockers and back packs. Hardcover editions of *It* and *Skeleton Crew* end up permanently missing from school library shelves. The King child protagonist addresses the problems of the child reader. Carrie White, for example, is a "nerd" who is teased at school by her peers and tormented at home by a fanatic mother, situations no doubt experienced by a number of teenage readers. Douglas Winter identifies King's comments on *Carrie*:

...Carrie is largely about how women find their own channels of power.... For me [King], Carrie White is a sadly misused teenager, an example of the sort of person whose spirit is so often broken for good in that pit of man—and woman-eaters that is your normal suburban high school.[15]

King returns to the high school setting in *Christine* with an equally harsh view towards the teenage "ghouls" who harass the introverted protagonist, and who ultimately become destroyed by the latent power of the introvert. For Carrie White, this destructive power is engineered *via* her telekinetic ability, and for nerd Arnie Cunningham, it is *via* his demon-possessed car. These two works function as revenge fantasies for the nerd who resides in each one of us. As teenagers, we have all felt persecuted by family or by friends or by the "system" itself. Carrie White and Arnie Cunningham illustrate a formulaic expression in King's horror fiction of this adolescent anxiety. Other tormented children populate his work: the young Ben Mears in *'Salem's Lot*, George in "Gramma," Danny Torrance in *The Shining*, and with these characters, the traditional elements of horror fiction aside, King challenges his adult readers to reexamine and reevaluate (and maybe remember) the actual hardships involved in growing up. For his young readers, he has become a type of popular clinical psychiatrist. He allows teenagers to face their problems in a fictional, non-threatening setting. In fact, King has become the spokesperson of the American teenager.

The enormous popularity of Stephen King as America's horror multi-media guru, in addition to his successful reworking of horror formulas with contemporary social melodrama, can be explained in another way. King himself did not spring full-grown from the collective mind of the American people, like an Athena from the skull of Zeus. There was a cultural context of horror stories in the history of American literature established before King, back long before his professional career, back before the decades of Ira Levin's *Rosemary's Baby* and William Peter Blatty's *The Exorcist*, before H.P. Lovecraft's dark fantasy pulp magazine fiction of the 1920s and 30s, before Robert W. Chambers' *The King in Yellow* (1895) and Ambrose Bierce's *Tales of Soldiers and Civilians* (1891) and *Can Such Things Be?* (1893), before the surrealistic short stories of New York bohemian Fitz-James O'Brien, before the gothic and psychological thrillers of Poe and the religious allegories of Hawthorne, before the "sketches" of Washington Irving, and yes, even before the dark, folkloristic ghost tales of the frontier pioneer. Truly, this American context of horror literature is an American tradition of horror. The American "dream" is really the American "nightmare"; unfortunately, many American culture scholars do not quite see it that way.

One of the continuing practices of these scholars since the turn-of-the-century is the quest to identify the monomythic American identity, as might be reflected in art and literature. Henry Nash Smith's *Virgin Land* (1950) and Richard Slotkin's *Regeneration Through Violence* (1973) focus attention on a national, literary identity founded on the American frontier experience. For other American culture scholars, the Algerian "rags-to-riches" myth (or the "American Adam" hero) is claimed as the symbol of our American-ness. Whatever else may be said of these insights into the mind and soul of a national character, certainly one prejudicial idea dominates: the notion that the American experience is a positive experience. A serious examination of American history (and the American popular literature that reflects that history) shows that nothing could be further from the truth.

For the European colonists, life in the New World was hell. The mortality rate, caused by disease, famine and a justifiably hostile native population, was high. Leisure time and a high standard of living were almost unheard of. The frontier pioneer and the plains farmer didn't have it any easier, working as hard and as fast as they could clearing trees and plowing the ground for crops, so they could merely survive. After industrialization, the life of the late nineteenth and early twentieth century factory worker was seemingly no better, with the long and dangerous working hours and the squalid urban living conditions. Not until the rise of the middle class (a relatively recent rise, for that matter) did the typical American standard of living go up, and the American mortality rate go down. As for the present, ask your neighbor about the day to day stresses of living, of the threat of terrorism, of nuclear war, of pollution, of income taxes and IRAs and the children's college education, and see what the answer might be. Well, American horror fiction in its many forms has charted this collective nightmare (and nearly every major American writer has tried his or her hand at the horror tale). With the advent of an information society, a mass mediated society, the horror genre has generated success in all perspectives of the media: film, television, print. And that reliable social barometer of the American subconsciousness, the mass media, measures the great degree of our infatuation with "things that go bump in the night." King has mastered this tradition, not invented it.

Before approaching King's definition and use of horror fiction formulas, an understanding of the cultural function of the horror story should be attempted. If we were totally rational about the way we view our existence, then it would seem obvious that we would make sane choices concerning our relationship with death. Death is an unknown. To the logical mind, if something cannot be defined, measured or understood, then it presents a serious, perhaps insurmountable, problem. The biological function of living has been charted by the scientist. Even the process of dying can be observed, tested and defined. But beyond that there exists a great, black veil, an oblivion that rational thought cannot explain, a place that cannot be observed, tested and defined. Our fear of death becomes intertwined with our uncertainty of the unknown, and thus fear of death translates into fear of the unknown.

Enter the belief system. We cannot it seems live without a direction or a purpose. We need something to tell us that we will be around the next day, the next year, the next forever. Most religions claim an afterlife, a place or a condition that we cannot see, a promise of purpose if only one "believes." Like religion, superstition is a belief system, but one that functions on a less complex, more primitive level. Superstition presents rituals of magic which predict or insure the outcome of the future without succumbing to the dogmatic burdens of religious ideology. Both religion and superstition are what can be termed the "irrational rational," or those ways of thinking which define something that otherwise is not definable. Horror fiction is a belief system, one that arguably operates much like religion and superstition (which would account, in part, for its popularity in all forms of mass media), and Stephen King senses this irrational rational quality in the genre.

The literary critic is presented a unique opportunity with King's work. Rarely does a popular author take the time to tell us how he writes: his creative methods, his theories of storytelling. Normally, he just lets his tales speak for themselves. In numerous interviews, in the introductions to several of his short story collections and especially in his book-length analysis of the multi-media horror genre, *Danse Macabre*, King has broken this unwritten tradition and has sketched for his readers the machinery of his fiction. For example, in the "Foreword" to the *Night Shift* collection, King suggests that there is an analogy between people who read horror fiction or view horror films and people who slow down their cars for a better look when they spot a terrible highway accident in the distance. King tells us:

The fact is—and most of us know this in our hearts—that very few of us can forego an uneasy peek at the wreckage bracketed by police cars and road flares on the turnpike at night.... No need to belabor the obvious; life is full of horrors small and large, but because the small ones are the ones we can comprehend, they are the ones that smack home with all the force of mortality.[16]

So King is outlining several points here. The first is that the reader is both attracted to and repelled by the content of the horror story, which ironically thus makes it a desirable type of entertainment, and the second is that the focus of the horror story is narrowed to the immediate personal experience. An axe-wielding murderer frightens us more than the possibility of a nuclear war since the one is more easily comprehended than the other. There is no rational reason why we buy and enjoy gruesome tales of death, or why we purchase theater tickets so that the cinematic "Jasons" can have their emotional way with us, but there is an irrational explanation that works, and King uncovers this explanation in *Danse Macabre*.

He defines a three level artistic function of the horror genre, and these divisions he terms the terror, horror and gross-out levels. To achieve "terror," which King calls the finest (or most artistic) of the three, this story must frighten without presenting any graphic violence. In other words, terror is the "unseen" scare. He claims that this type of story is the most difficult for an author to write. King's second level of the horror genre he terms "horror." The horror tale is not "entirely of the mind," hence it is less artistic: it shows the reader the viscera of violence, the face and form of the evil monster. And finally for King, his third level is the "gross-out," which involves the reader's gag reflex. This least artistic division is the most primitive in its intentions: a desire to make one ill with a spectacular display of gore.[17] Utilizing these three divisions in his work, King states:

My own philosophy as a sometime writer of horror fiction is to recognize these distinctions because they are sometimes useful, but to avoid any preference for one over the other on the grounds that one effect is somehow better than another...and so I will try to terrorize the reader. But if I find I cannot terrify him/her, I will try to horrify; and if I find I cannot horrify, I'll go for the gross-out. I'm not proud.[18]

King also suggests that horror fiction is allegorical or symbolic: "Horror appeals to us because it says, in a symbolic way, things we would be afraid to say right out straight...it offers us a chance to exercise...emotions which society demands we keep closely in hand."[19] The symbolic expression of the horror genre, for King, divides into two basic areas: larger, cultural fears and smaller, personal fears. Cultural fears include such things as the fear of invasion, which he identifies in the films *Invasion of the Body Snatchers* (1956) and *Earth vs. the Flying Saucers* (1956). Regarding personal fears, King nicely surveys those in his essay, "The Horror Writer and the Ten Bears." He borrows the word "bears" from Joseph Stephano, screenplay writer and producer of the 60s SF/horror television program, *The Outer Limits*, who used the term to indicate the show's inclusion of a monster each episode. King says: "It's a good term for the aspiring writer of horror fiction to use, because it gets across the idea that general phobias have to be focused on concrete plot ideas before you can hope to scare the reader."[20] King's ten bears are 1) fear of the dark; 2) fear of squishy things; 3) fear of deformity; 4) fear of snakes; 5) fear of rats; 6) fear of closed-in places; 7) fear of insects (especially spiders, flies, beetles); 8) fear of death; 9) fear of others (paranoia); and 10) fear *for* someone else.[21]

Interestingly, King's fiction oftentimes exhibits a differing quality that is not part of his defined genre levels or his symbolic cultural and personal functions. One of his lesser known short stories, "The Man Who Loved Flowers," from the *Night Shift* collection best illustrates this quality.

The man, or protagonist, in "The Man Who Loved Flowers" is unnamed. The reader is given a succession of trite, sentimental vignettes as substance for the story's plot, but of course King is positioning us for a fall, a morbid joke. The setting—a May, 1963 evening in New York City—is described in mawkish language: the air is "soft and beautiful"; the man is stereotyped as looking like a young lover. The vignettes are established, one after the other, as the young man walks by a series of onlookers. We are given the onlookers' impressions of the man. He is wearing a light gray suit. His hair is cut short; his complexion is fair; and his eyes are a light blue: "He had that look about him," that look of love thinks the first person he passes, who is an old lady carrying two bags of groceries. She considers him to be beautiful. The young man pauses at a handcart filled with flowers for sale. The proprietor of the handcart, an old man also thinking the young man to be in love, sells him tea roses. A radio is blasting "out bad news that no one is listening to," news about the hammer murderer and war and world politics. The young man walks on. Other people watch him go by, a traffic cop and two women smoking and talking outside a "washateria." He finally turns down a "narrow lane," off of a street that is a "little darker" than the rest, and he approaches a young woman. We at last enter the young man's mind. King is about to deliver the punch-line of his little joke.

Smiling, the young man calls to the woman, calls her Norma (an interesting connection made here to Robert Bloch's psychopathic protagonist of Psycho, Norman Bates) and notices—for the reader as well as for himself—that it's a surprise seeing how young the woman looks. The surprise, of course, is not just the young man's: it will be the reader's, King foreshadowing his joke. As he moves closer to "Norma," his smile trembles; her smile fades. It's getting dark and her face blurs. He hands her his flowers and says " 'Norma.' " The woman thanks him and answers that he must be mistaken, that her name is.... And the young man replies " 'Norma.' " as he withdraws a short-handled hammer from his coat pocket and does her in. King's punch-line delivered, the balance of the story briefly relates the young man's background: a serial killer, we discover, who has murdered five other "Normas." He swings his hammer for two reasons: first, to stop "Norma's" scream and second, to demonstrate his...love, that he is in love, that "his name [is] love." And as the story concludes, he cleans his hammer, returns it to its hiding place in his coat and continues walking, a "bounce" appearing in his stride. Observed by a middle-aged couple, the woman turns to her husband and asks why he doesn't have that look of love anymore, that look that the young man so obviously possesses, and when her husband replies with a dumbfounded " 'Huh?' " she says to him: " 'Nothing' " and thinks "that if there [is] anything more beautiful than springtime, it [is] young love."

In "The Man Who Loved Flowers," as in a good deal of King's fiction, the reader is played with, manipulated, teased, shown a scenario that looks like it's all sunshine and saltbox houses with picket fences. King, then, gives the reader a sharp slap to the face, and the reader's vision changes. The sunshine darkens quickly as if a thunderstorm is on the way. The paint on the saltbox houses cracks and peels and blisters; the picket fences rot and amazingly, the reader wipes the crust from the collective eyes and says: I see it clearly now. The houses are skulls and the fences are jagged teeth.

The young man who loved flowers does not. He loves death. King clouds all of his characters' perceptions in the story, even the victim's, with sunshine and saltbox houses with picket fences. The "lover," as seen by the others (including, at first, the reader as well) is the killer. The flowers are a gruesome mask for his real gift: the deadly hammer. The reader is shocked, entertained, but now possesses a clearer vision of life. King smiles at a job well done.

And thus for King, the horror lies not so much with the monsters but with a faulty perception of the monsters, seeing them as something that they're not, something harmless or innocent. King frames this message in his fiction as an extended joke. So you think Carrie White is a nerd? Surprise! She's a force of powerful destruction. So you think that nice doggie is cute. Surprise! It's a killer St. Bernard. So you think that car can be pretty sharp with some work. Surprise! It's Christine, and it (she) has a taste for blood. So you think that mist over the lake is harmless. Surprise! It's the forerunner of mankind's apocalypse. So you think nurses are supposed to be healers, are supposed to be helpers. Surprise! You have yet to meet Annie Wilkes. For King's readers, the insidiousness of the SURPRISE is heightened because he wants us to "feel" for his characters:

You have got to love the people [characters]. See, that's the real paradox. There has to be love involved, because the more you love—kids like Tad Trenton in *Cujo* or Danny Torrance in *The Shining*—then that allows horror to be possible. There is no horror without feeling. If you have that, then horror is possible, because horror is contrasting emotion to our understanding of all the things that are good and normal. Without a concept of normality, there is no horror.[22]

The final punch-line of King's extended joke is the twisting of the normal into the abnormal, and the horror of it all is when people fail to perceive this change of reality, and are consequently destroyed by their lack of vision. King's joke is indeed a dark jest.

It's fitting to conclude this discussion of King by introducing a discussion of his most recently published novel, *Misery*. This book can easily be described as a watershed effort, as a pause in breath of America's nightmare storyteller. It's a thinly veiled self-examination of his fans, his writing and his genre work. In his essay entitled "On Becoming a Brand Name," King identifies himself as a producer (and a product) of horror fiction who is known for his product—a brand name author. King says:

I would define a 'brand name author' as one who is known for a certain genre of the popular novel—that is, Robert Ludlum is the Bird's Eye of neo-Nazi spy suspense, Helen

MacInnes is the Listerine of ladies' 'international intrigue' stories, John Jakes is the General Motors of popular American historical fiction, and I, perhaps, am the Green Giant of what is called the 'modern horror story.'[23]

Well, this so-called Green Giant of the modern horror story is mired in a paradox, and *Misery* expresses the popular author's plight of, on the one hand, recognizing the commercial success of being a brand name author, and, on the other hand, the literal "misery" of being typecast into writing only a certain genre novel.

Misery is the story of Paul Sheldon (the writer of popular historical romances featuring the heroine Misery Chastain) who becomes involved in a serious auto crash during a snow storm in an isolated region of Colorado. He is discovered and revived by a psychopathic ex-nurse named Annie Wilkes. She takes Paul to her out-of-the-way farm where she keeps him doped-up on narcotics. Paul's legs are twisted and broken beyond all hope, and he's in a great deal of pain. Paul became involved in the accident because he was so excited about his new fictional effort, a realistic novel that totally breaks tradition with his Misery Chastain series (which he has come to despise). Annie, when she saves Paul, quickly discovers that he is the author of the Misery novels, and she thinks of herself as his number one fan of the character. What the psychopath Annie soon learns, however, is that Paul (having tired of his bestselling character and killing her in his last book) is attempting to change direction with his literary life. This overwhelms what little sanity she possessed in the first place, and the remainder of King's novel chronicles Annie's continued imprisonment and torture of Paul as she forces him to revive his despised character, Misery, and write a new adventure for her.

The inside dust jacket blurb claims that *Misery* is a love letter to King's fans. Hopefully, the writer of that blurb is being facetious. *Misery* is more like hate mail, as a survey of some of King's comments, spoken *via* the Paul Sheldon personna, shows. Paul thinks to himself in Section I of the story:

No, Annie, he thought, suddenly filled with fury. *I'm no whore. Fast Cars was about not being a whore. That's what killing that goddamned bitch Misery was about, now that I think about it. I was driving to the West Coast to celebrate my liberation from a state of whoredom. What you did was to pull me out of the wreck when I crashed my car and stick me back in the crib again. Two dollar straight up, four dollar I take you around the worl.*[24]

King at this point views the genre writer (and himself) as a whore, and brand name fiction writing as a state of whoredom. Annie is the symbol of his following, slavish to the brand name product and totally intolerant to change. Annie destroys Paul's serious novel, *Fast Cars* (the only copy he had) perhaps as King's readers destroy his attempts at breaking new ground. To encourage his dependence, and his revival of Misery, Annie seduces Paul with drugs (money for King?) and violence: a foot chopped off here, a thumb amputated there. Paul literally sacrifices his body for his number one fan, and King no doubt at times feels the same way figuratively. But as Paul is hounded and tortured and brainwashed into writing the new Misery novel, his very attitude about writing the genre story changes. He even starts to justify it. Towards the conclusion, King writes:

So what was the truth? The *truth*, should you insist, was that the increasing dismissal of his work in the critical press as that of a 'popular writer' (which was, as he understood it, one step—a small one—above that of a 'hack') had hurt him [Paul] quite badly. It didn't jibe with his self-image as a Serious Writer who was only churning out these shitty romances in order to subsidize his (flourish of trumpets, please!) REAL WORK! Had he hated Misery? Had he really? If so, why had it been so easy to slip back into her world? No, more than easy; blissful, like slipping into a warm bath with a good book by one hand and a cold beer by the other. Perhaps all he had hated was the fact that her face on the dust jackets had overshadowed his in his author photographs, not allowing the critics to see that they were dealing with a young Mailer or Cheever here—that they were dealing with a *heavyweight* here. As a result, hadn't his 'serious fiction' become steadily more self-conscious, a sort of scream? *Look at me! Look how good this is! Hey, guys! This stuff has got a sliding perspective! This stuff has got stream-of-consciousness interludes! This is my REAL WORK, you assholes! Don't you dare turn away from me....*[25]

The author's voice is tormented here. It's a passionate moment in the novel. King is wrestling with his perceptions of what constitutes good and bad writing. Paul reconciles himself with his genre work at the novel's end and survives. Maybe King has done the same.

Naturally the thing that Paul Sheldon and Stephen King fear the most is the CRITIC: the critic Annie who slices away another part of the body when Paul fails to follow her literary expectations, or the critic *New York Times* book reviewer who lambastes the new King novel as it rockets its way up the bestseller list. King's view of his work and his view of the critics' view of his work are an amazing blend of self-depreciating humility and arrogance. *This* collection of essays about King and his writings, if nothing else, suggests that King's moment for critical recognition has arrived. The following essays approach their subjects in different ways, but are arranged for the reader from the general, contextual examination of the horror genre to the specific examination of King and his work.

For example, Carol Senf's paper, "Blood, Eroticism, and the Vampire in Twentieth-Century Popular Literature," suggests that the vampire engenders sympathetic treatment in popular literature today because it represents a form of freedom in life style and sexual preference. The blood motif, which is downplayed these days, is probably not as ghastly in our society as it has been in the past because of everybody's familiarity with blood-banks and transfusions. Senf makes the interesting point that the relatively tame and loving activities of vampires compare favorably with the horrendous acts that mankind performs against the well-being of mankind.

Garyn Roberts, in his paper "Of Mad Dogs and Firestarters—The Incomparable Stephen King," introduces us more precisely to King and his works. But Roberts is careful to show that King, although very individual in his treatment of his stories, stands knee-deep in the traditions of his predecessors.

In the next essay, "Reading Between the Lines: Stephen King and Allegory," Bernard Gallagher expands on one aspect of King's work which readers must keep in mind if they are to get the full impact of his accomplishment—its allegorical approach. According to Gallagher, King's first level of allegory is the "gross out," that level, as Gallagher says, "at which a cultural norm is violated for shock effect." King's second level is that at which his probing, instead of seeking out the supernatural levels turns instead to the "political, economic and psychological." This approach provides a key to unlock profound insights into American and general life.

In "A Blind Date With Disaster: Adolescent Revolt in the Fiction of Stephen King," Tom Newhouse glosses one of the insights found behind the door of allegory. To him King's fiction is about and for adolescents and teen-agers as it traces the effects of a corrupt culture on a vulnerable level of society. That level runs amuck and rebels against that culture and society, and King is their spokesman and secretary.

In "Freaks: The Grotesque as Metaphor in the Works of Stephen King," Vernon Hyles examines another aspect and function of King's fiction, that of the grotesque as metaphor in present-day society. The "new Gothicism," as Hyles defines it, has three characteristics: it is an "expression of the estranged or alienated world"; it is a play against the absurdities of existence; it is an effort to exorcise and control the demonic elements in the world. King builds in and on these assumptions with dramatic results.

In "Viewing 'The Body': King's Portrait of the Artist as Survivor," Leonard Heldreth explores the examination of the physical element in King's stories, and he concludes that by translating the archetypal aspects of life, "King and other writers help to break down the loneliness of life and even of death."

James Hicks continues exploring the beneficial aspects of King's works in "Stephen King's Creation of Horror in 'Salem's Lot: A Prolegomenon Towards a New Hermeneutic of the Gothic Novel." The beneficial effect, Hicks says, comes through confrontation: " 'Salem's Lot creates horror as it brings its readers face to face with themselves, and they discover the horror of themselves."

Linda Badley's "Love and Death in the American Car: Stephen King's auto-Erotic Horror" is a two-ton essay about the permeating fixation of love and death in the American car. A survey of the subject, the paper puts King's works in the driver's seat with a heavy foot on the gas pedal.

Centering on *The Dark Tower*, James Egan's "*The Dark Tower*: Stephen King's Gothic Western" combines three distinct genres—the Western, the Gothic and the Apocalyptic fable—and in so doing "evokes the Western rather than obliterating it."

In demonstrating that King is a writer to be taken very seriously, Samuel Schuman, in "Taking Stephen King Seriously: Reflections on a Decade of Best-Sellers," uses *Pet Sematary* as his test case. Schuman demonstrates that King has four major strengths: "a surprisingly effective prose style"; "an ability to create characters at once unique and universal"; "a strong and clear ethical stance"; "an ability to imagine and represent plots which is absolutely brilliant." King's works, in Schuman's words, constitute "an imaginary toad in a real garden."

In another examination of *Pet Sematary*, Mary Ferguson Pharr, in "A Dream of New Life: Stephen King's *Pet Sematary*," contends and demonstrates that King's novel carries on the thesis of Mary Shelley's *Frankenstein*, saying that: "The nexus between the two novels—between their centuries, in effect—occurs in the dream of new life each presents, a dream both seductive and malefic, the stuff finally of nightmares made flesh."

In the final two essays in this collection the authors use *Pet Sematary* to reach out into yet other generalities. Tony Magistrale, in "Stephen King's *Pet Sematary*: Hawthorne's Woods Revisited," ties in the book with Nathaniel Hawthorne's allegories of sin. Magistrale posits about King: "How his characters react to the loss of innocence is a central theme in King's work; their ability to survive is dependent upon what they learn from the fall from grace."

Natalie Schroeder's essay, " 'Oz the Gweat and Tewwible' and 'The Other Side': The Theme of Death in *Pet Sematary* and *Jitterbug Perfume*", takes us to the final act of life, a theme which has haunted us in all the papers, death. King's message on the subject, in Schroeder's words: "We must work to overcome our fears of death, for dying is a natural process which no one can defeat." In these two books, Robbins transmutes his fears into something else: "a humorously fantastic tale, replete with philosophical theories, pornographic scenes and outrageous puns," while King translates "the horrifying supernatural events into a cathartic preview of our own forthcoming battles with death."

In all, these essays, although obviously not covering all aspects of King's fine and provocative works, cover most of the obvious ones and provide suggestions for other areas of study. There can be no doubt that King is a remarkable phenomenon of our time. It is time that he be as appreciated by scholars as by the general reading public. This volume of essays is, we hope, only the first of many which will further elaborate on King's role in American literature today.

Notes

[1] Stephen King, "On Becoming a Brand Name," *Fear Itself: The Horror Fiction of Stephen King*, ed. Tim Underwood and Chuck Miller (San Francisco: Underwood-Miller, 1982), p. 28.

[2] Walter Arnold, "America's Reading," *Mass Media and the Popular Arts*, ed. Fredric Rissover and David C. Birch (New York: McGraw-Hill, 1983), p. 218.

[3] Stefan Kanfer, "King of Horror," *Time*, CXXVIII (October 6, 1986), 74-75.

[4] Ibid., p. 74.

[5] Douglas E. Winter, *Stephen King* (San Bernardino: Borgo Press, 1982), p. 9.

[6] Douglas E. Winter, "Talking Terror: Interview with Stephen King," *The Twilight Zone Magazine*, V (February 1986), 18.

[7] Winter, *Stephen King*, p. 9.

[8] King, "On Becoming a Brand Name," pp. 16-19.

[9] Ibid., pp. 19-20.

[10] Douglas E. Winter, "Collecting King," *The Twilight Zone Magazine*, V (February 1986), 32-33.

[11] Ibid., p. 97.

[12] Ibid., p. 32.

[13] Kanfer, p. 83.

[14] Stephen King, "Children of the Corn," *Night Shift* (New York: New American Library, 1978), p. 250.

[15] Winter, *Stephen King*, p. 33.

[16] Stephen King, "Foreword," *Night Shift* (New York: New American Library, 1978), p. xv.

[17] Stephen King, *Danse Macabre* (New York: Berkley, 1981), pp. 21-23.

[18] Ibid., p. 25.

[19] Ibid., p. 31.

[20] Stephen King, "The Horror Writer and the Ten Bears," *Kingdom of Fear: The World of Stephen King*, ed. Tim Underwood and Chuck Miller (New York: New American Library, 1986), p. 12.

[21]Ibid.

[22]Winter, "Talking Terror," p. 22.

[23]King, "On Becoming a Brand Name," p. 15.

[24]Stephen King, *Misery* (New York: Viking, 1987), p. 66.

[25]Ibid., pp. 263-264.

Blood, Eroticism, and the Vampire in Twentieth-Century Popular Literature

Carol A. Senf

Sterling O'Blivion in *I, Vampire* (1984) by Jody Scott, introduces herself with a bizarre confession: "To remain young and adorable, I must drink six ounces of human arterial blood once a month. This is not an ethical choice. I was born this way. If society wants to kill or cure me, that's not up to me."[1] She adds that she has had this condition for seven hundred years, but she offers no apologies, no complaints.

If O'Blivion is reconciled to her condition, the neurotic Smith in Charles Beaumont's "Blood Brother" (1963) complains to his psychiatrist about his state and the diet that prolongs it: "I always used to like my steaks rare, but *this* is ridiculous! Blood for breakfast, blood for lunch, blood for dinner. Uch—just the thought of it makes me queasy to the stomach!"[2] Even worse is the violence he is compelled to commit: "Do you think I *enjoy* biting people? Do you think I don't *know* how disgusting it is? But I tell you, I *can't help it*.... And because of it, everybody hates me!"[3]

Smith's unhappy existence is ended by the psychiatrist, who stabs him with a wooden letter opener, but the narrator in Robert Bloch's "The Bat is My Brother" (1944) must conclude his story with an impassioned plea for the reader to bring the stake that "represents release and peace."[4]

Despite their obvious differences, these three characters are vampires, creatures from primitive folklore that are nonetheless familiar to most twentieth-century readers of popular literature. Familiar with the more or less attractive vampires in these recent versions, readers may be surprised to discover that vampires in the past were not nearly as appealing as these three characters. In fact, few modern versions do justice to the hideousness of Bram Stoker's physical description of Dracula, a characterization that adapted various folklore accounts:

20

The mouth, so far as I could see it under the heavy moustache, was fixed and rather cruel-looking, with peculiarly sharp white teeth; these protruded over the lips. . . . For the rest, his ears were pale and at the tops extremely pointed. . . . As the Count leaned over me and his hands touched me, I could not repress a shudder. It may have been that his breath were rank, but a horrible feeling of nausea came over me, which. . . I could not conceal. (Ch. II)

Resembling a bat more than a human being in this scene, Stoker's character even smells of his unsavory habits. Despite the gruesome physical description, however, *Dracula* (published 1897) was a turning point for the literary vampire. Earlier literary versions—including *Varney the Vampire*, Polidori's *The Vampyre*, and "Carmilla" had presented the vampire as a hideous creature; and Stoker's central character is often more attractive than he is here. Indeed Stoker sometimes reveals him as no more cruel than his human opponents. Following Stoker's lead, twentieth-century writers often portray the vampire as a more sympathetic character than he had been in either folklore or literature.

At the same time that vampires become more attractive (in literally every sense of the word—attractive physically, morally, and intellectually), their human counterparts become more horrifying. For example, Hans Heinz Ewers (1871-1943), who wrote "The Spider," a literal vampire story of a beautiful woman who destroys the men who love her, also wrote *Vampir* (1921), in which the word "vampire" is used metaphorically. In *Vampir*, Frank Braun, a young German patriot during World War I, drinks the blood of his Jewish mistress to become a better fund raiser for his country. By comparison, Clarimonde, the beautiful vampire in "The Spider," is much less horrifying for she is directly responsible for the deaths of only three men.

Ewers in *Vampir*, Manley Wade Wellman in "The Horror Undying" (1936) and David Drake in "Something Had To Be Done" (1976) reveal human evil that puts the vampire's bloodthirsty nature into a less horrifying perspective. "The Horror Undying" takes place in the American West, where the violence of the vampire is unpunished for a long time, primarily because people attribute it to hostile Indians. In fact, Wellman portrays a cruel period in our nation's history when he reveals that Sergeant Stanlas has a brilliant military career before he is revealed as a vampire *and* a cannibal. Drake's story, on the other hand, presents a more recent horror, for he has his story take place in Viet Nam. During a three-week period, the vampire—Stefan Lunkowski— destroys five men before his sergeant, Morezek (a man whose Old World origins apparently permit him to recognize a vampire even in a war zone), rolls a grenade into his bunk. Morezek then returns to the States, where he destroys Stefan's family and himself with another grenade.

Emphasizing the cruelty that is so often a part of war, Drake reveals that Morezek himself is dying of skin cancer, probably the direct result of exposure to Agent Orange, a chemical now linked to cancer, skin disease, and other disorders among Viet Nam veterans. At the beginning of the story, Morezek mentions, "We were out in the middle of War Zone C.... No dinks, no trees—they'd all been defoliated."[5] The real horror of Agent Orange makes the vampiric Lunkowskis appear less horrifying.

Along the same lines as Wellman and Drake, Ronald Chetwynd-Hayes's *The Monster Club* (1975) indicates that vampires and other supernatural monsters are actually less aggressive and destructive than human beings. He has one of his monsters, a ghoul, draw the human character's attention to recent history to emphasize the horror of *human* aggression:

In the past sixty years the humes [or humans] have exterminated one hundred and fifty million of their own kind.... The humes began with many serious disadvantages, but these they overcame with wonderful ingenuity...they invented guns, tanks, aeroplanes, bombs, poisonous gas, extermination camps, swords, daggers, bayonets, booby-traps, atomic bombs, flying missiles, submarines, warships, aircraft-carriers, and motor-cars.... During their short history they have subjected other humes to death by burning, hanging, decapitation, electrocution, strangulation, shooting, drowning, racking, crushing, disembowelling and other methods too revolting for the delicate stomachs of this assembly.[6]

Although no more violent than human beings, the Lunkowskis, Sergeant Stanlas, and the characters in *The Monster Club* are not necessarily attractive characters. Other twentieth-century writers, however, have created vampires that are considerably more appealing. For example, Anna in "Softly While You're Sleeping" (1961) finds the vampire, Mr. Varri, much more appealing than her would-be human lovers because he doesn't attempt to force his advances on her:

Her body relaxed into trembling quietness...even before she felt the prickle of the two tiny sharp teeth gently piercing the thin skin, gently drawing out her blood and, with it, her fears and anxieties and self-doubts. This *is* love, she thought wonderingly as her throat swelled to meet the vampire's kiss—a true kiss, not the clumsy suction of damp lips and the thrust of slimy tongue, not the disgusting fumble of sweating, odorous human bodies.[7]

Ultimately Anna recognizes that her love for the courtly and gentle Varri will result in her death, so she finally decides to relinquish her vampire lover.

An equally attractive vampire is Miriam in *The Hunger* (1981) by Whitley Strieber. Beautiful, cultured, and intelligent, Miriam is the daughter of Lamia and, therefore, a member of an entirely different species. Hungering for the life of her human victims, which she absorbs by drinking their blood, she is horrifying. However, realizing that the centuries old vampire is the last of her kind, readers may be so touched by her appalling loneliness that they sympathize with her search for someone to share her immortality.

Creating even more sympathetic vampires are Jan Jennings, George R.R. Martin, Les Daniels, Chelsea Quinn Yarbro, and Fred Saberhagen. Jennings entirely removes the threat from the vampire's bloodsucking habit. In *Vampyr* (1981), Valan, an extremely attractive woman vampyr (her preferred spelling), who has never tasted human blood, leads an equally civilized group in punishing the "rogues" that prey on human beings. Joshua York, the humane vampire in Martin's *Fevre Dream* (1982), wants to save his race from their predatory habits and devotes three years of his life to discovering an acceptable substitute for human blood. Both Daniels and Yarbro reveal that their vampire characters are appalled by human treachery and violence. Don Sebastian de Villanueva in Daniels" *Citizen Vampire* (1981) is sickened by the violence he sees during the Reign of Terror and disgusted by the Inquisition in *The Black Castle* (1978) and the activities of the Spanish conquistadors in *The Silver Skull* (1979). Similarly in *Hotel Transylvania* (1978), Yarbro deliberately contrasts the vampire and bloodthirsty human beings when the human Madelaine writes to her vampire lover:

> In my reading of history there is war and ruin and pillage and lives snuffled out with such profligacy that my breath is stopped by the senselessness of it. One would think that all humanity had nothing better than to feed on its own carrion. I have thought as I read these books, how many much worse things there are in this world than vampires.
>
> To know your freedom. To live in the blood that is taken with love.
>
> Saint-Germain, Saint-Germain, I can hardly wait![8]

According to Yarbro's interpretation, the vampire is no longer a cruel mirror of mankind's worst violence, but a cultured outsider who observes and comments on this cruelty. Tracing Saint-Germain's activities from ancient Egypt, to the Roman Empire, to Renaissance Italy, to Enlightenment France, and finally to twentieth-century England, she places him in situations where his urbane behavior contrasts sharply with the senseless cruelty of human beings. As a result, Saint-Germain becomes more sympathetic by comparison.

Twentieth-century writers have used a number of strategies to make their vampire characters more attractive than their predecessors in folklore or earlier fiction. Chetwyn-Hayes, Daniels, and Yarbro, for example, reveal that vampires are less bloodthirsty than ordinary human beings; Wellman and Drake put the vampire's violence into historical perspective and reveal that the vampire is no more cruel than human beings; Scott, Strieber, and Anne Rice in *Interview with the Vampire* (1976) and *The Vampire Lestat* (1985) present its unorthodox behavior sympathetically, Rice especially showing the vampires' desire to know and experience rather than merely to destroy human beings; Richard Matheson, in *I Am Legend* (1954), reveals that vampires are the result of plague; Jennings and Martin totally eliminate the horror from its behavior; and finally writers have permitted their vampires to tell their own stories. *I, Vampire* and Saberhagen's *The Dracula Tape* (1975) are both first-person accounts; and, like Grendel in John Gardener's retelling of *Beowulf*, the "monsters" in many of these works are extremely compelling. Jaded by the commercialism of the twentieth century, Sterling O'Blivion is attractive, both in her extreme honesty and in her desire for a less violent world:

And can the Inner Core [a C.I.A. type of group that has her under surveillance] help the poor twerp any more? Not at all!, not even as the supremely powerful Intersystem that it is, with a finger shoved up each of the world's intelligence orgs, moving their heads and arms, like the Punch and Judy dolls I hated as a child in Europe. I hated it when they whacked each other with clubs! The other children all howled in delight. The *normal* children—which may tell you something.[9]

Like Yarbro, Scott reveals that ordinary human behavior is both frightening and cruel. The vampire, an oppressed outsider who is frightened by this ordinary behavior, thus becomes less horrifying by comparison. Equally compelling is Dracula in Saberhagen's series. *The Dracula Tape*, the first novel in the series, retells Stoker's novel from Dracula's point of view and directs the reader's attention to certain inconsistencies in Stoker's novel. In the following passage, Dracula explains that he was not responsible for Lucy Westenra's death:

Lucy I did not kill. It was not *I* who hammered the great stake through her heart. *My* hands did not cut off her lovely head, or stuff her breathless mouth—*that mouth*— with garlic, as if she were a dead pig....Only reluctantly had I made her a vampire, nor would she ever have become a vampire were it not for the imbecile Van Helsing and his work.[10]

The astute reader of the two novels will remember that Dracula is correct in his assessment; and the rest of *The Vampire Tape* continues to vindicate the vampire. As a result Saberhagen's Dracula is an appealing figure while his human opponents appear to be both stupid and brutal.

Somewhat less appealing are the first-person accounts in "Conversion" (1976) and "The Bat is My Brother," in which narrators reveal their horror when they discover that they have died and been reborn as vampires. However, even here, seeing the events from the vampires' point of view makes these twentieth-century vampires considerably more attractive than their merely bestial predecessors in folklore, who were victims of their uncontrollable hunger for human blood.

More attractive than their predecessors, twentieth-century vampires do remain bloodsuckers even though Saberhagen, Yarbro, Jennings, Martin, and other writers manage to eliminate most of the horror from this trait. In addition, some twentieth-century works alter the original superstition and make blood sucking a metaphor. For example, the unnamed subject of Fritz Leiber's "The Girl with the Hungry Eyes" (1968) is neither literally dead nor literally a bloodsucker although Leiber is obviously aware that the traditional vampire is a corpse that destroys the souls of its victims by drinking their blood. Thus he makes his human subject (who finally comes to symbolize the false promises of modern advertising) more deadly than the supernatural vampire:

There are vampires and vampires, and the ones that suck blood aren't the worst.... She's the smile that tricks you into throwing away your money and your life. She's the eyes that lead you on and on, and then show you death. She's the being that takes everything you've got and gives nothing in return.[11]

In Leiber's story, although the word "vampire" is a metaphor rather than a literal belief, it is no less deadly.

In addition to sucking blood, a number of vampires rebel against authority. The unnamed woman vampire in Everil Worrell's "The Canal" (1927) refuses to acquiesce to any kind of authority, and she sneers at the narrator's offer of assistance:

'Do you think you would be helping me, to tie me to a desk, to shut me behind doors, away from freedom, away from the delight of doing my own will, of seeking my own way? Rather this old boat, rather a deserted grave under the stars for my home!'[12]

Accustomed to admiring this kind of romantic independence, many readers are likely to see this refusal to conform to arbitrary social standards as attractive, but the narrator reveals that his lovely vampire has purchased her freedom for an awful price, for she is a child murderer.

More attractive, though equally deadly, is Erich in "Night Life" (1976) by Steven Utley, a rebel against a corrupt twentieth-century society who preys on other less attractive rebels. Coming to America from Europe he chooses to prey on the "muggers, hookers, pimps, pushers, rip-off artists, two-bit con men, low-priced killers-for-hire. In the nights to come, he would come to know them all better."[13]

Finally, a rebel against authority in a more recent work is Juliette (based on Sade's novel of the same name) in *Citizen Vampire* (1981). She and Sade, who makes a brief appearance, are libertines, defined as "Society's criminals, and nature's heroes."[14] Eager for new sensations, she revives Don Sebastian, a centuries old vampire, who becomes her lover and turns her into a vampire to help her escape the guillotine. However, Juliette, who has rebelled against the authority of her husband, the monarchy, and the revolution, is incapable of following the restrictions required of vampires either. Thus, when her grave is discovered by the young woman who had been her personal servant before the revolution, she is destroyed.

Many vampires in twentieth-century literature are portrayed as blood suckers or rebels, but the single trait that distinguishes almost all of them is their overt eroticism, a characteristic that is generally presented as a positive trait. For example, Mr. Varri, the vampire in Smith's "Softly While You're Sleeping" is a tender, solicitous lover even though his courtship would ultimately result in Anna's death. Both Miriam in *The Hunger* and Valan in *Vampyr* are described as sensuous and physically ardent; and, like Sterling of *I, Vampire*, both have taken numerous lovers of both sexes. Moreover, while Miriam and Sterling do require human blood to sustain their existence, neither they nor Valan are dangerous because of their eroticism.

Other twentieth-century vampires seem to take definite delight in their sexuality, some even being characterized as polymorph perverse. For example, Dracula and the other vampires in Saberhagen's novels (*The Dracula Tape*, 1975; *The Holmes-Dracula File*, 1978; *An Old Friend of the Family*, 1979; and *Thorn*, 1980) clearly take erotic pleasure in their relationships with "breathing human beings." The same pleasure applies to Saint-Germain and his followers in the novels of Chelsea Quinn Yarbro (*Hotel Transylvania; The Palace*, 1978; *Blood Games*, 1979; *Path of the Eclipse*, 1981; and *The Saint-Germaine Chronicles*, 1983).

The vampire in the twentieth century is certainly not a consistent character, but there are some definite family resemblances. The one trait that links them all is their need to drink blood although many twentieth-century writers have eliminated the horror from this characteristic by letting the vampire substitute animal blood or by reducing the amount that is required. (In addition, many writers have eliminated another horrifying aspect by making the vampire a member of a different species instead of a reanimated corpse.) For example, Sterling's need for six ounces of human blood a month hardly seems excessive; and the fact that she, St. Germaine, Saberhagen's Dracula, and Valan do not need to kill for this blood makes them even less monstrous. In addition, the twentieth-century vampire is often rebellious—sometimes violent in the rebellion against the society that has rejected him or her. Saint-Germain, for example, rebels against the societies in which he lives and continues his scholarly quest for a better world. Less attractive vampires, on the other hand, simply reject the human world with which they are forced to coexist. Finally, the twentieth-century vampire is almost always an erotic creature. In fact, eroticism is so much a part of the vampire's character in the twentieth century that it is easier to mention the few exceptions to this rule: The timid Smith in "Blood Brother;" the brutal Sergeant Stanlas in "The Horror Undying;" Stefan Lunkowski in "Something Had to Be Done"; and the dogs in *Hounds of Dracula* (1977) are the only examples of vampires in twentieth-century popular literature for whom brute strength is more important than seduction.

Looking back over these examples of twentieth-century literary vampires reveals one striking fact about the vampire today. Although the sheer number of vampires in the twentieth century reveals that the vampire remains an important mythic figure (and therefore a figure worthy of serious study), it is undoubtedly a character of popular literature rather than of serious literature and drama—a creature that stalks pulp fiction as well as the films, television programs, paperback books, and comics of the modern world. (It would be possible to cite numerous other examples; Raymond T. McNally's bibliography in *Dracula Was a Woman* cites more than a hundred and fifty individual entries—novels in vampire series, individual vampire novels, and short stories—although McNally is not overly scrupulous about distinguishing vampires from their near relatives—werewolves, zombies, and human beings who resemble the vampire.[15] There are exceptions, such as Anne Rice's *Interview With The Vampire* (1976), a book that was taken seriously by literary critics as well as enjoyed by members of The Literary Guild, and its sequel *The Vampire Lestat* (1985), but the exceptions merely prove the rule.

Moreover, the vampire in the twentieth century—more often than not—is an attractive figure. (Here too are exceptions, of course, such as Barlow in Stephen King's immensely popular *'Salem's Lot* (1976);[16] and Dracula in *Sherlock Holmes vs. Dracula* (1978) by Loren Estleman; Prince Conrad Vulkan in Robert R. McCammon's *They Thirst* (1981); and Jerry Dandrige in *Fright Night* (1985) by John Skipp and Craig Spector; but many of them are little more than clones of Stoker's Dracula with a little folklore thrown in for good measure.) The vampire in popular literature today is more likely to resemble Yarbro's urbane St. Germain, Saberhagen's witty Dracula, or the pensive Miriam in *The Hunger* than the bestial figure from folklore.

In the twentieth century, writers who have featured the vampire have focused on the individual's right to choose a different kind of existence, especially when that alternative does not cause harm to other individuals. Thus there has been increasing emphasis on the positive aspects of the vampire's eroticism and on his or her right to rebel against the stultifying constraints of society. In fact, recent writers have emphasized their vampires' desires for peaceful coexistence with human beings.

As a result, most twentieth-century interpretations of the vampire have been more light and playful than their counterparts in folklore or earlier literature. Though the trend is certainly worthy of more attention than can be given in a short article, this greater tolerance is undoubtedly the result of a growing acceptance of variations in individual behavior. In fact, Margaret L. Carter comments specifically on this growing toleration when she observes that the vampire is no longer "the universally feared and hated villain of nightmare tradition":

Increase in knowledge of psychology and sociology no doubt contributes to the change in attitude. Today we no longer feel qualified to judge any man...as a monster. Current emphasis on minority problems may even cause a monster to be an appealing character, because he suffers for being "different." Furthermore, moral ambiguity is more acceptable in this century than the last; we are less apt than Stoker to consign any creature to irrevocable damnation. There is also the simple artistic problem of an overworked plot motif. Too many imitations of the "Dracula" pattern must inevitably pall on the reader.[17]

Carter is undoubtedly correct about the reasons for this increasing toleration, not to mention simple boredom with a literary motif that has become a cliche. Formerly monsters to be feared, both because of their sexual preferences and their bloodthirsty habits, vampires in twentieth-century popular literature are often presented as appealing figures rather than as threats.

Recently a few writers have introduced vampire figures who are as menacing as their predecessors in folklore and nineteenth-century literature. Included in this group are Jerry Dandridge in *Fright Night* or the hideous Dolores in Jorge Saralegui's *Last Rites* (1985). The vampires in these recent works have none of the appeal of the vampires in most other twentieth-century works. *Fright Night* features a truly despicable vampire who feeds on the blood of prostitutes and who turns the young hero's best friend into a vampire also while *Last Rites* features a cadaverous old woman who will do anything to preserve her existence.

Since the vampire in popular literature has evolved over the years, it is tempting to draw an analogy between the present social and political climate (especially the renewed strength of fundamentalist religious groups, the associated tendency toward sexual repression, and the belief that once again authority of whatever kind signifies right) and the fact that the vampire—almost always an erotic being and a rebel against authority—is once again perceived as a threat. However, two books do not alter the trend that has made the vampire an appealing figure in twentieth-century popular literature. Formerly monsters to be feared, both because of their sexual preferences and their bloodthirsty habits, vampires remain appealing figures; and the rare exceptions to this trend do not necessarily mean that the pendulum is swinging away from a greater acceptance of human differences to a hatred and fear of perceived differences. It is simply too soon to tell.

Notes

[1]Jody Scott, *I, Vampire* (New York: Ace Science Fiction Books, 1984), p. 13.

[2]Charles Beaumont, "Blood Brother," in *The Rivals of Dracula: A Century of Vampire Fiction*, ed. Michel Parry (London: Corgi Books, 1977), p. 165.

[3]Beaumont, p. 165.

[4]Robert Bloch, "The Bat is My Brother," in *The Rivals of Dracula*, p. 162.

[5]David Drake, "Something Had To be Done," in *The Rivals of Dracula*, p. 169.

[6]Ronald Chetwynd-Hayes, *The Monster Club* (London: New English Library, 1975), pp. 189-90.

[7]Evelyn E. Smith, "Softly While You're Sleeping," in *The Curse of the Undead: Classic Tales of Vampires and Their Victims* (Greenwich, CT: Fawcett, 1970), p. 189.

[8]Chelsea Quinn Yarbro, *Hotel Transylvania* (New York: Signet, 1978), p. 278.

[9]*I, Vampire*, p. 130.

[10]Fred Saberhagen, *The Dracula Tape* (New York: Warner, 1975), p. 7.

[11]Fritz Leiber, "The Girl with the Hungry Eyes," in *The Midnight People*, ed. Peter Haining (New York: Popular Library, 1968), p. 205.

[12]Everil Worrell, "The Canal," in *The Undead*, ed. James Dickie (New York: Pocket Books, 1976), p. 199.

[13]Steven Utley, "Night Life," in *The Rivals of Dracula*, p. 177.

[14]Les Daniels, *Citizen Vampire* (New York: Ace Fantasy Books, 1981), p. 58.

[15]Raymond T. McNally, *Dracula Was A Woman: In Search of the Blood Countess of Transylvania* (New York: McGraw-Hill, 1983), pp. 215-244.

[16]King admits that he was consciously reworking *Dracula*, as Douglas E. Winter explains in *Stephen King: The Art of Darkness* (New York: New American Library, 1984):

'Salem's Lot was written in 1973; the idea resulted from a dinner conversation in which King, his wife, and his long-time friend Chris Chesley discussed what might happen if Dracula returned in modern times, not to London, but to rural America. When King jokingly said that the FBI would quickly put him to rest, a victim of wiretaps and covert surveillance, his companions noted that almost anything could occur unnoticed in the small towns of Maine, (pp. 36-37)

After mulling over the idea, King did decide to set his modern vampire tale in a small town in Maine.

There is, however, one big difference in Dracula and 'Salem's Lot, which is noted by Gregory A. Waller, The Living and the Undead: From Stoker's Dracula to Romero's Dawn of the Dead (Urbana: University of Illinois Press, 1986): "King is much less optimistic than Stoker about man's ability to unite in a moral community that will triumph once and for all over the undead and so become the basis for a regenerated existence in the twentieth century" (p. 249).

[17]Margaret L. Carter, Shadow of a Shade: A Survey of Vampirism in Literature (New York: Gordon Press, 1975), p. 126.

Of Mad Dogs and Firestarters—
The Incomparable Stephen King

Garyn G. Roberts

In the last fifteen odd years, Stephen King has not only revolutionized the world of popular literature, he has taught us—onlookers, consumers, and critics alike—a thing or two about ourselves as individuals, and as members of a larger world culture. For King himself is a product of his individual experiences and cultural inheritances, and he mirrors what we are all about.

To date, not the most prolific of wordsmiths, King is the most commercially successful author of all time. Each new King novel or short story collection becomes a multi-million copy seller, and is destined to rise to the top of the *New York Times* Bestseller List in a few short weeks. "In little more than ten years, some fifty million copies of his books have been sold worldwide and thirteen motion pictures have been based on his work," stated Douglas Winter in 1985.[1] And frightening, in more ways than one, is that Stephen King is only forty-years-old (b. September 21, 1947) and has a literary career ahead of him that boggles the mind. His "art of darkness" has just begun.[2]

But, how original is the Dark Fantasy of Stephen King? John G. Cawelti suggests in his *Adventure, Mystery and Romance* (1976) that popular stories are a carefully crafted balance of convention and invention, or extended from that idea—fact and fantasy, the old and the new. It follows then that there is a degree of newness and freshness in King's tales of the macabre. And, there is an element of the old.... No, the very old—the ancient. Precisely what are the conventions and inventions of this contemporary grandmaster's electric prose?

Stephen King came about as a "brand name" largely because the culture in which he emerged created, produced, and nurtured him. The tales that have been burned into the typewritten page and word processor computer disk, and ultimately bestselling novel, at the hands of King stem from a heritage of horror. In the mid-nineteenth century, there was Edgar Allan Poe; in the early twentieth—Howard Phillips Lovecraft;

31

and in the waning years of the twentieth—Stephen King. And, there were, are and will be others before, in between and after. King did not just come around; he's been centuries in the making. The definitive survey and study of the Horror genre in the mass media—King's own *Danse Macabre* (1979)—is not just a wonderfully insightful and profound study of Dark Fantasy, it is King's own dissection of his heritage of horror. Douglas Winter, the number one biographer of King with the obvious exception of King himself, has produced further works that substantiate the notion of King as an outgrowth of a heritage of horror. These are, most notably, *Stephen King: The Art of Darkness* (1984), and his (Winter's) interview with King published in *Faces of Fear* (1985).

About his early writing King notes, "I would have short stories where I started off sounding like Ray Bradbury and ended up sounding like Clark Ashton Smith—or even worse, they would start off as James M. Cain and end up as H.P. Lovecraft."[3] King was, and is, an avid student of those who preceded him in his field. Particularly in the case of the 1930s "Weird Tales" published in the pulp magazine with the same name (the golden age for this the most important publication of dark fantasy and weird fiction), King finds fodder for his literary soul. In the fifties, that period in which the master found himself in his impressionable childhood, the science fiction/horror movies of the day like *The Thing* (1951) and *The Creature From the Black Lagoon* (1954) had particular impacts on his future writing, as did the emergence of the new American art form called "Rock 'N' Roll." The fifties and sixties also showcased Richard Matheson's and Rod Serling's teleplays for *The Twilight Zone* for the aspiring author. These people and events, and more, became the foundation for the house of King.

Both the novels and short stories of the Stephen King canon evidence a number of old traditions and time-tested themes which have manifested themselves in modern forms. Ray Bradbury's *Dark Carnival* (1947) (later cut to about two thirds its original length in *The October Country* (1955)) provided, and provides, a harvest of dark fantasy and weird fiction which has long been imitated and emulated in the work of King. Emerging from Bradbury's Dark Carnival mythos was the novel *Something Wicked This Way Comes* (1962), and there were his novels *Fahrenheit 451* (1953) (where firemen burned books!) and *The Martian Chronicles* (1950) (perhaps the "Best" piece of science fiction ever done). There were also those wonderfully twisted tales of the macabre collected in books of the always underrated, but consistently excellent Robert Bloch, and later, 1959's *Psycho* by Bloch (from which, of course, Alfred Hitchcock and Tony Perkins have reaped a rather macabre immortality). In addition to Bradbury, to a degree, King's work evidences remnants of the work of H.P. Lovecraft, Robert E. Howard (King's "Gunslinger" stories are straight out of the Heroic Fantasy of Howard), and Clark Ashton Smith—the three musketeers of *Weird Tales*. And, there were others. King notes, "In college, I would go around with a John D. MacDonald book, or a collection of short stories by Robert Bloch, and some asshole would say, 'Why are you reading that?' and I'd say, 'Hey, this man is a great writer.' "[4] But, he adds, "The guy who taught me to do what I am doing is Richard Matheson...."[5] Richard Matheson...along with Robert Bloch, Ray Bradbury, and Fredric Brown—the most underrated American author of the twentieth century. While Matheson is most often remembered for his contributions to *The Twilight Zone* television program, where he, Rod Serling, and Charles Beaumont were the primary creative forces, Matheson also produced the landmark novels *I Am Legend* (1954) and *The Incredible Shrinking Man* (1956)—an existential trek into oblivion where death is the welcomed end.

The heritage of horror that produced and embraced all the aforementioned people and events goes back even further. In fact, like many popular culture forms, stories of horror and the supernatural can be traced back to folklore, and even further, the earliest recorded beginnings of man. For it is death and after-life, and stories of the same, which have been man's most basic concern since the dawn of time. In folklore, two particular motifs in such stories have been prevalent. These are "The Hook Story" and "Tales of the Tarot." In fact, King himself addresses these influences in *Danse Macabre*. From the latter, the earliest examples of stories of vampires, werewolves, and nameless abominations appeared. King has retold all three of these "tales of the tarot" in his work.

Yet, where specifically are Bradbury and company reincarnated in the King canon? King's first bestseller, *Carrie*, appeared in 1974. Douglas Winter notes, "*Carrie* is largely about how women find their own channels of power, and what men fear about women and women's sexuality...."[6] Along with Brain De Palma's movie adaptation of the novel, *Carrie* launched King's popularity. The novel, and movie, are essentially a portrayal of the physical and psychological horrors of adolescence. Carrie, herself, however, does not experience the "normal" metamorphosis so often equated with this awkward human transformation. She is abused by her mother and classmates—home and society—alike, the same affliction that haunted Frankenstein's monster, various and assorted vampires (vampyres)—Dracula included, and the werewolf (wehr-wolf).

Speaking of vampires, in *'Salem's Lot* (1975), King recreates the classic vampire story, focusing on a town full of vampires rather than one isolated member of the living dead. Here, he also throws in the terrors of the haunted house, which, as in Edgar Allan Poe's "The Fall of the House of Usher," represent the horrors and inner workings of individual and collective minds alike. The Marsten house in *'Salem's Lot* is a great house that serves as a central symbol of the town in which it rests, and further, the individual and social mind alike. The haunted house motif in Stephen King's work only begins here. This motif is enhanced and is the basis for King's first hardcover bestseller—*The Shining* (1977). In this story, the Overlook Hotel is that house. Haunted houses have been the forte of gothic stories for centuries, as in Horace Walpole's *The Castle of Otranto* (1764), and Poe's nineteenth century tale of the house of Usher. In contemporary literature, before the work of King there were also Richard Matheson's *Hell House* in 1971 (which King acknowledges as a major influence on *The Shining*) and Shirley Jackson's *The Haunting of Hill House* (1959), and so on. The reason however, that the haunted house story, and the horror story in general works, and King mentions this in several places, is that the reading audience feels an empathy for and affinity with the person or people caught in the house. In *The Shining*, we feel an affinity with young Danny Torrance who is trapped in the structure which has driven his family to madness.

Maybe the height of Stephen King's literary career to date came with the appearance of *The Shining* and the novel which followed shortly thereafter—*The Stand* (1978). *The Stand* turned out to be a leading contender for the title of best Stephen King novel. Douglas Winter explains the events that lead to *The Stand*...

He [King] was haunted by a news story that he had read about an accidental chemical/biological warfare spill in Utah that had nearly endangered Salt Lake City; it reminded him of George R. Stewart's science fiction novel *Earth Abides* (1949), in which a plague decimates the world. One day, while listening to a gospel radio station, he heard a preacher repeat the phrase "Once in every generation a plague will fall among them." King liked the sound of the phrase so much that he tacked it above his typewriter....[7]

Winter deems *The Stand* an epic fantasy much in the realm of Tolkien and E.R. Eddison. *The Dead Zone* (1979), a political horror novel followed, and again the central idea, in this case political horror and intrigue, was a time tested storyline. Dino De Laurentiis' production values, Christopher Walken's performance in the starring role of English teacher Johnny Smith, and Martin Sheen's portrayal of the megalomaniacal politician Greg Stillson in the movie of the same name, made this, without doubt, the best film adaptation of a King novel to date.

Ray Bradbury turned out *Fahrenheit 451* in 1953 and King produced *Firestarter* in 1980. More than similar storylines tied these two works together. Both were released in limited edition asbestos covers, as well as mass market editions. "In 'The Mist' " (a King novella originally appearing in Kirby McCauley's edited horror collection *Dark Forces* and recently reprinted in *Skeleton Crew*), Stephen King conjures the quintessential faceless horror: a white opaque mist that enshrouds the northeastern United States (if not the world) as the apparent result of an accident at a secret government facility," claims Douglas Winter.[8] This, of course, is reminiscent of King's own work in *The Stand*. Years before *The Stand*, however, faceless horrors similar to the "white opaque mist" in "The Mist" scourged the earth's population in popular fiction. William Hope Hodgson (1887-1918), accomplished World War I hero for England, built several of his Sargasso Sea stories and other such fantasies around this notion of a faceless mist, fog, or wind. Ray Bradbury's "The Wind" (a classic 1943 Weird Tale) is a perfect example of this.

It's a big cloud of vapors, winds from all over the world...I know its feeding grounds, I know where it is born and where parts of it expire. For that reason, it hates me, and my books that tell how to defeat it. It doesn't want me preaching anymore. It wants to incorporate me into its huge body to give it knowledge. It wants me on its own side![9]

John Carpenter directed the motion picture *The Fog* in 1980 and Dennis Etchison wrote the novelization for the same, and the list of other precedents for "The Mist" goes on and on.

Two of King's more recent dark fantasies, *Cujo* (1981) and *Cycle of the Werewolf* (1983), are retellings of the classic werewolf story.[10] Both breathe new life (or death?) into this very old storyline. The title character of *Cujo* is a mad dog. There is not the exact form of transformation of human to beast that is characteristic of the old werewolf story. But, *Cujo* certainly is derivative of that archetypal storyline in other ways. As the title of *Cycle of the Werewolf* suggests, the focus of this King work (which is indeed a treasure when coupled with the magnificent illustrations of Berni Wrightson) is a dissection and discussion of the transformation process the human/werewolf entity experiences according to ancient folklore.

Pet Sematary (1984) is in some ways King's most horrifying tale because the terror extends beyond mere human death as we know it; it deals with the mysteries of the after-life. George Romero and John Russo, director and writer of *The Night of the Living Dead* movies and books which have endeared themselves to more than a cult following in the sixties, seventies, and eighties, are surely an influence on *Pet Sematary*. Again, other precedents for King's work exist. His recent novel *It!* (1986) is an affectionate tribute to all the monsters that have haunted the movie screen, mass market novel and other popular media for decades.

The heritage of horror from which Dark Fantasy's contemporary grandmaster draws is perhaps self evident. And, King is the first to acknowledge all those creators, writers, monsters, media that have fed his literary soul. Yet, it would be only part of the larger picture if we claimed that this heritage of horror is the sole explanation for King's success (in our hearts as well as in publishers' bank accounts). There is indeed an inventional aspect to the works—no, masterpieces—of King. Essentially, these inventions come in two forms. First, there is King's successful updating of old themes, and his ability to recontextualize the "horrors" of the Horror story for a contemporary audience. King has poured his life experiences, as an individual and as a member of a larger culture, into his stories. And, as a regular, decent guy, he recounts adventures we can all relate to. We haven't personally seen a werewolf or a vampire, but King's conception of these are the same as ours. We know that when we meet that werewolf or vampire, it will be exactly as King has described them. Second, there is King's dexterity with the English language that few, if any, can match. While he claims to have no identifiable, conscious style, King has made the vernacular equal "Art." He told Douglas Winter, "I always wrote for myself, and then I looked for a market that was somewhere in the ballpark of what I was doing."[11] That ballpark was, and is, the American, and now world, public.

Notes

[1]Douglas E. Winter, ed., *Faces of Fear* (New York: Berkley Publishing Group, 1985), p. 236. Since 1985, several additional movie adaptations have been produced.

[2]Douglas Winter's terminology.

[3]Winter, p. 243.

[4]Ibid, p. 247.

[5]Ibid, p. 244.

[6]Douglas E. Winter, *Stephen King: The Art of Darkness* (New York: New American Library, 1984), p. 33.

[7]Ibid, p. 55.

[8]Ibid, p. 86.

[9]Ray Bradbury, "The Wind" in *Dark Carnival* (Sauk City, Wisconsin: Arkham House Publishers, 1947).

[10]*Cycle of the Werewolf* was retitled *Silver Bullet* when the movie adaptation of the novel was released.

[11]*Faces of Fear*, p. 238.

Reading Between the Lines: Stephen King and Allegory

Bernard J. Gallagher

Without a doubt, Stephen King is the one popular novelist whose earnings and reputation have undergone a horrifyingly meteoric rise. In 1982 King pocketed two million dollars for all of his works (Gray 87); in 1986 he pocketed three million dollars alone as an advance on his novel, *It* (Bangor-Kanfer 74). In 1982 he had almost forty million books in print (Gray 87). In 1986 he had over sixty million books in print (Bangor-Kanfer 74). In 1982 *Time* magazine's Paul Gray claimed that King represented a threat to serious book lovers everywhere. In 1986 *Time* magazine's Stefan Kanfer and Cathy Booth-Bangor aim no poison darts at King and his works. At worst their breezy and irreverent style implies a critical attitude toward King and his works." At best, they attempt both to explain the tradition of horror fiction and to locate King within the context of that tradition.

Time magazine's shift in attitude, to some degree, reflects a corresponding shift in the halls of libraries, high schools, and colleges. I don't mean to suggest that King is about to replace Shakespeare. I do, however, want to suggest that a cultural phenomenon of such proportions deserves scrutiny. Moreover, I want also to suggest that a good number of the readers, fans, and critics of Stephen King, as do *Time's* reporters, ignore what eventually may be regarded as the most important book in the King corpus, *Stephen King's Danse Macabre*. This book of quasi-criticism not only brings an interesting and sometimes incisive critical vision to the work of horror, it also reveals an implicit critical method which opens up a realm of interpretive possibilities for popular fiction, film, and television. What I propose to do, then, is to clarify King's discussion of critical method in his *Danse Macabre* and then demonstrate how this method might apply in both close readings of a particular text and in general interpretations of popular cinema and television.

The insight which King offers into the work of horror is based upon a bimodal or dualistic vision which insists upon the necessity of reading between lines. The first mode or level which King describes is the "gross out" level—i.e., that level at which a cultural norm is violated for shock effect (4). Examples of the gross out include Reagan's vomiting in the priest's face in *The Exorcist* or the monster in Frankenheimer's *The Prophecy* crunching off a helicopter pilot's head (4). The second and subtextual level—the between the lines, so to speak—he describes is the artistic level (4), that is, a second level at which horror novels seek to probe "phobic pressure points" (4) which address archetypal, "political, economic, and psychological rather than supernatural fears" (5). Examples of this second and artistic level include the fear of death implicit in *Ghost Story* (262), the xenophobia implicit in Christopher Nybey's *The Thing* (152), and "economic unease" in *The Amityville Horror* (142). This second level, according to King, gives the work of horror its "pleasing allegorical feel" (5).

At this point, things become much less straightforward. King offers us little help in defining and understanding what he means by "pleasing allegorical feel." On one occasion, King treats allegory as a "symbolic way" of saying "things that we would be afraid to say right out straight" (31), a way for readers to "exercise emotions which society demands we keep closely in hand" (31). On another occasion he refers to the preceding notion of allegory as subtext or the "liaison formed between" our fantasies and our real fears (129). On still another occasion he talks about "symbols" and "symbolic mirrors" in general (144). And on other various occasions, he mentions "archetypes" (57) and "mass dreams" (144). Clearly, the pleasing allegorical feel about which King speaks has little to do with the allegory of the Middle Ages. The phrase, as he applies it, does not offer a system of symbology that extends and operates in the fashion of *The Pearl* or *The Romance of the Rose*. It is not a multi-modal system of symbols which offers the possibility of simultaneous interpretations on the literal, moral, anagogical, and allegorical levels.

Instead, the "pleasing allegorical feel" about which King speaks is a peculiar kind of psychological allegory, for the readings between the lines to which King invites us invariably discuss the political, social, and economic anxieties of the contemporary individual. For example, *Carrie*, according to King, is actually a feminist novel which confronts a young woman's psychic conflict when she attempts to live as a strong and autonomous individual in a culture that would prefer to see her as a passive and powerless piece of femininity (172). Moreover, *The Amityville Horror*, according to King, is really a story of economic unease which traces the demise of a young couple who buy a home they can't afford (142).

Once we recognize that King's bimodal vision of allegory places extraordinary emphasis upon hidden psychological anxieties or upon reading between the lines, we begin to see that a surprising number of parallels exist between the structure of King's allegory and the structure

Freud attributes to the dream. These parallels deserve our attention not so much because they correspond in an overly neat and academic way but because they help clarify King's interpretation of critical method and because they suggest the possibility that this critical method has universal applications.

Freud divides the dream into two basic levels of meaning just as King divides the work of horror into the levels of the gross out and subtext. The first and most obvious level of meaning in a dream, according to Freud, is the manifest or dream content-level (218). Physical experiences as recalled by the memory comprise this level. In other words, remembered movements, colors, sensations, and experiences compose the dream's first level of meaning. The second level of meaning in a dream, according to Freud, is the psychic or latent content level. Desires springing from the unconscious comprise this second level (218;238). These desires, of course, invariably involve the wish-fulfillment of an infantile sexual impulse (495).

Both the systems of Freud and King, then, are bimodal. Moreover, both men argue that their bimodal systems result from the need of the individual to generate a superficial level of meaning which will disguise or hide a deeper and more disturbing level of meaning. King writes that horror fiction allows us to say "things that we would be afraid to say right out straight" (31), and Freud argues that the psyche creates the manifest content of the dream to "evade censorship" and to allow the dreamer to continue to sleep while expressing his suppressed and potentially disruptive desires (485). The schemes of both King and Freud, then, operate on the assumption that the surface level in either the work of horror or the dream generates its symbolic structure in order to protect the individual from the internal conflicts which he finds disruptive.

This need to disguise the latent or deeper content of the work of horror and the dream, of course, serves to separate further the psychological allegories of Freud and King from medieval allegory. Medieval allegory did not exist as a means of protecting the individual from disruptive truths. Instead, it existed as a conscious artifice which allowed the individual to manufacture and to understand a multi-modal vision of life which emphasized both the physicality of the here and now and the reality and importance of the spiritual. The allegories of King and Freud, meanwhile, frequently result from the unconscious attempt of the contemporary individual to cope with and yet hide from disruptive wishes and experiences. In short, both men use the concept of allegory to explain a kind of psychological ambiguity which results from the individual's desire to remain relatively safe and comfortable when confronting any of the many unpleasant truths of the human condition.

Once we see that the bimodal visions of King and Freud arise from the beliefs of both men that individuals find it necessary to disguise the latent or allegorical contents of their works, we can find one more impressive parallel. The writer of the work of horror and the dreamer apparently rely on the same three basic principles of condensation, transference, and displacement (338) when choosing the material which will comprise both the manifest level and the disguise of the story or dream. King, of course, makes no direct reference to any of these terms, but he skillfully employs the concepts of condensation, transference, and displacement when he interprets the movie, *The Amityville Horror*. King begins his interpretation by employing the Freudian notion that the dreamer, (in this case you may substitute director), condenses or compresses into an everyday incident a hidden anxiety or wish. He argues that "everything which *The Amityville Horror* does well is summed up in" (143) a single scene which depicts a financial crisis: a brother-in-law loans $1,500 that he does not have to a newly-wedded bridegroom. On the basis of this scene alone, King goes on to argue that *The Amityville Horror* is really a movie about "economic unease" (142). In turn, King supports this hypothesis of "economic unease" by transferring to this everyday event—"Gee, honey I'm overdrawn at the bank"—an intensity which did not originally belong to it. Of course, this transference to an everyday event of intensity which does not belong to it is the very thing that Freud describes with his term, transference (338). In order to sustain this interpretation of "economic unease," King must also employ the Freudian concept of displacement, for he argues that the everyday incident of the overdraft at the bank holds a second and more important meaning than we would normally assign it (338).

Only three significant divisions, then, lie between King and Freud and their bimodal visions. The first and most obvious difference lies in how transference occurs in the work of horror. Normally, transference means that an individual has transferred to an everyday incident an intensity which does not belong to it. However, a work of horror apparently reverses this operation by using an unusually intense event as a way of obliquely referring to the horror inherent in an everyday act too disturbing to discuss openly. In effect, then, the work of horror provides a vehicle for the metaphoric expression of terror at some everyday event which normally masks its horribleness behind a mundane face. Second, King, unlike Freud, does not locate the Oedipal triangle and its obvious emphasis on sexual competition between the offspring and the parent of the same sex at the center of his allegorical system. Instead, he suggests, under the headings of archetype and symbol, that a variety of interpretations are available to the individual interested in the work of horror. There are the universal fears of death, sexuality, and dark nights, and there are everyday fears about money, complexion, politics, and the slightly odd next-door neighbor. Third, King, unlike Freud, does not reduce every work of horror to an infantile impulse. Consequently, the interpretive possibilities in King's system of allegory are less reductive than the interpretive possibilities in Freud's system.

In spite of the fact that King is not a Freudian, the parallels which exist between his critical vision and Freud's are important. The Freudian concepts of manifest and latent content, condensation, transference, and displacement help to define King's critical method of reading between the lines. More importantly, though, the similarities between King's method of interpreting the work of horror and Freud's universal method for interpreting dreams imply that King's critical method has applications extending far beyond the work of horror. In fact, King's method for reading between the lines may be applied with great success to popular fiction, film, and television.

For instance, we do not need to scrutinize Ludlum's *The Bourne Identity* too closely in order to discover that it possesses the "pleasing allegorical feel" about which King speaks. On the gross out or manifest level, the novel traces the odyssey of David Webb, alias Jason Bourne, who has experienced a total loss of memory while in the middle of a counter-insurgency spy mission designed to draw out and destroy the super assassin, Carlos. On the artistic or subtextual level, though, the novel explores the problem of human identity. In short, it asks the same question Christopher Lasch asks in his book, *The Minimal Self: Psychic Survival in Troubled Times*: has the invasion of "culture and personal life by the modern industrial system produced...a loss of autonomy...[and] a tendency to confuse self-identification with the exercise of consumer choices" (41-42). Lasch's answer is a resounding yes. According to him we live in a narcissistic culture, that is, a culture in which the individual, like the Narcissus of Greek Myth, can no longer clearly distinguish between himself and his environment. Ludlum's answer to the question is also a resounding yes; and he, too, suggests that the individual who is self-reliant has at least a slight chance at independence and personal identity.

We can easily begin to support the notion that *The Bourne Identity* symbolically explores the problems of personal identity in an indifferent, or perhaps even hostile, technological world by first identifying, as did King and Freud, the incidents and characters in which everything the novel does well is "summed up" (King 143). And without a doubt, the novel's protagonist, David Webb, provides us with a perfect example of King's summing up and Freud's condensation. When Webb, alias Jason Bourne, nearly drowns at the outset of the novel, we encounter what I consider to be the key to understanding the story's subtextual discussion of the perils of personal identity.

He felt rushing cold water envelope him, swallowing him, sucking him under...And there was heat, a strange moist heat at his temple that seared through the freezing water that kept swallowing him...he felt these things, acknowledging his own panic as he felt them. He could see his own body turning and twisting, arms and feet working frantically against the pressures of the whirlpool...yet strangely there was peace. It was the calm of the observer, the uninvolved observer, separated from the events....Then another form of panic spread through him....He could not submit to peace. Not yet. (14)

What you've just read, on the manifest level or the level of the gross out, is the description of the near-drowning of David Webb after he has been wounded and washed overboard into a stormy sea. This near drowning, however, takes on new significance when we read the comments made by Doctors Washburn and Panov. Washburn clearly establishes Webb as a sort of white Anglo-Saxon everyman when he describes Webb as "the prototype of the white Anglo-Saxon people seen everyday on the bitter cricket fields, or the tennis court" (22). At the conclusion of the novel, Doctor Panov expands Washburn's guess at Webb's everyman role when he says, "In a way, he's [meaning Webb] a functioning microcosm of us all. I mean, we're all trying to find out who the hell we are, aren't we?" (522) In short, Ludlum has condensed contemporary man into the character of David Webb.

Moreover, since the novel deals with the problems of an amnesiac everyman trying to discover his true identity, we also realize that the whirlpool and storm which threaten Webb represent much more than the far-reaching horrors of immediate drowning. At the subtextual level, in fact, these two elements of natural destruction actually serve as metaphoric expressions of the individual's desire to relinquish his personal identity. What tempts Webb is not the agony of drowning at sea but the peace that follows the abandonment of the struggle to survive. And what nearly kills Webb is not the sea itself but the calm detachment which renders him apathetic to his condition. Once we realize that the storm and the whirlpool have only drawn out attitudes that were already present, we also realize that the emphasis in this particular scene resides not in the physical presence of the sea but in Webb's psyche. And since Webb functions as an everyman, we also realize that we supposedly share in the same psychic weaknesses. Consequently, we can then see evidence of the transference to which King indirectly refers in his interpretation of *The Amityville Horror*, a way of intensely expressing our fears of losing our identities. Reading between the lines as King would, we also see, then, that a displacement has occurred and that Webb's temptations and near-drowning metaphorically express the contemporary American's temptations to abandon the struggle for personal identity in favor of the calm and peace of the unobtrusive and minimal self (Lasch 33-36).

Once we establish the subtextual concern of *The Bourne Identity* with the temptations and problems faced by the individual interested in developing an authentic personal identity, nearly every incident in the novel refashions and repeats the opening crisis of the near drowning in chapter 1. Indeed, Ludlum seems to run Webb through a checklist of institutions in order to demonstrate the inability of any institution to form an authentic personal identity. For instance, the novel opens with a "Preface" which offers two seemingly authentic news releases about the shadowy figure, Carlos. As we read through both releases, we see that in both instances these newspapers offer very little real information. In fact, the only thing about which we can be sure is that the newspapers are not sources of hard information or personal identity. Later on in the novel, Marie St. Jacque—the romantic interest—confirms our suspicions about newspapers when she says:

"Both [stories] are constructed out of lies, the first connected to the second by tenuous speculation—public speculation—on a banking crises that would never be made public.... And that second story—the patently false statement that millions were stolen from Gemeinschaft—was tacked onto the equally false story that I'm wanted for killing three men in Zurich. (278).

Newspapers in Ludlum's *The Bourne Identity* are sources of misinformation and are, therefore, incapable of aiding the individual in understanding either himself or his world.

The Bourne Identity, however, is democratic in its criticism. It not only damns the press, it also damns the military industrial complex and the United States government. In spite of an incredible amount of planning and an equally incredible amount of secrecy, the United States Government's plan to trap Carlos falls apart because government officers, due to circumstances beyond even their control, can no longer make sense of what has happened to Webb (292). Not only did their scenario fail to consider the possibility of Webb's injury, it also failed to consider Webb as a human being. Consequently, they are invariably puzzled by Webb's actions, largely because he has forgotten the identity they manufactured for him and has begun to act according to a set of internal values that emphasize love and loyalty. Furthermore, once Webb begins to operate consistently on a set of values, he also begins to abandon his chameleon-like identity for an identity which is both personal and authentic.

Ludlum's criticism of institutions as potential sources of personal identity extends beyond newspapers and government to include even the sacred cows of banking and medicine. For instance, Webb begins his search for identity at a bank in Zurich, believing somehow that the factual nature of his relationship with the bank will help him overcome his amnesia. Ironically, just the opposite happens. Once in the bank, Webb mistakes his alias, Jason, for his real name. He also wrongly surmises that the codename, Treadstone, is the name of a business firm for which he works. He also mistakenly believes that Mr. Koenig, an employee of the bank is trustworthy. At the root of these three mistakes, however, we find one truly serious mistake, that is the assumption that a bank and money can somehow help him discover who he is. Although the newspapers, government, and Swiss Bank are all venerable institutions promoting the established order, they cannot then, provide our everyman with an authentic identity.

Doctors and medicine are also inadequate sources of the individual's identity—they are far too materialistic and quantitative. However, both Doctor Washburn and Doctor Panov seem to understand that their profession is limited and that the individual alone must be the source of his personal identity. Washburn warns Webb early on that the task he is about to undertake is not easy and that he alone must be the source of his identity. He says:

"I think I know what's going through your mind. A sense of helplessness, of drifting without a rudder to put you on course. I've been your rudder, and I won't be with you; there's nothing I can do about that. But believe me when I tell you, you are not helpless. You will find your way." (35)

Washburn's metaphor of the ship and rudder, of course, harkens back to the opening metaphors of the sea and the whirlpool in chapter one, and his statement is essentially a reaffirmation of Webb's earlier decision to brave the storm and whirlpool rather than to abandon himself to the whims of circumstance. Panov, at the end of the novel, makes a similar kind of assertion. He says:

I've too much respect for the human mind to deal you chicken soup psychology; there's too damn much of it floating around in the wrong hands.... It's true we can go in with a knife a reach the storm centers, reduce the anxieties, bring a kind of peace to him. Even bring him back to what he was, perhaps. But it's not the kind of peace he wants...." (522)

In other words, Washburn and Panov both recognize that authentic personal identity resides not in institutions but in the individual and his attempts to confront the turmoil of life. Indeed, Ludlum's novel,

The Bourne Identity, and Christopher Lasch's book, *The Minimal Self,* both seem to advise us that authentic personal identity resides not in the lobotomized peace of a minimal and chameleon self but in the tension and struggle of the individual to balance his individuality against the claims that nature and society make upon him.

I have only managed to offer you a little of what Ludlum has sandwiched between the lines of his popular novel, *The Bourne Identity.* However, I believe it is sufficient to show how we can apply King's method of allegorical interpretation to popular works of spy fiction as well as to popular works of horror. I will now provide you with a few more samples of how we may apply King's method of allegorical interpretation to popular film and television. Without any particularly strenuous effort, we can find any number of popular American films that offer the same sort of political, economic, and social allegories that King found in horror fiction. The recently released summer film entitled, *Short Circuit,* for instance, offers three major subtextual or allegorical possibilities.

On the manifest or gross-out level, it traces the picaresque adventures of a military robot, who because of an unexpected jolt of lightning to his circuitry, leaves the confines of the factory and undertakes an educational journey into the surrounding countryside. On the subtextual level things become more complicated. First and foremost, the movie satirizes the technological mind that attempts to reduce the world to stimulus response or to a vision of input and output. Eventually, the technocrats in the film must learn from a misplaced flower child that life necessarily involves relationships and emotions.

Second, but hardly less important, the film satirizes the tendency of the military-industrial complex to turn everything bright and beautiful into an unthinking purveyor of destruction. The delightful little robot has value for the military so long as he is a mechanism without emotion. Once he begins to function as a human being and to remind the human beings in the movie about the importance of humor, love, and plain old silliness, he loses any value he has for the military. In short, the film offers a comic but critical commentary on the notion that a good citizen is a good soldier who does what his country asks without question.

Third, the film offers a humorous indictment of American materialism with its portrayal of the martini-drinking but ineffectual scientist turned administrator. Thus, this apparently harmless little film offers in its blithe way encouragement to the American who feels insecure in his social role and uncomfortable with the recent bellicosity exhibited by his government. The uneasiness of Americans, however, does not always translate into movies criticizing society. Indeed, popular movies seem to just as often serve to support the *status quo*. Consider, for instance, the not-so-recent film *Splash.*

A seemingly harmless and irrepressible comedy, *Splash* does everything within its power to set the women's movement back into the fifties. A brilliant woman-mermaid (she learns English in no more than a couple of weeks), conventionally beautiful with her long blonde hair and svelte figure, and sexually insatiable, pursues the male romantic lead, who is puckish but not particularly handsome or intelligent. Clearly, the mermaid represents essentially the same vision of woman that we could find in the *Playboy* magazines of the fifties. The movie, however, does soften its sexist edge when the male character willingly relinquishes his earthly life for a life of love beneath the sea. However, even this last gesture does little to mute the film's sexism; for it clearly implies that a fantasy life with a fantasy woman as defined by conventional male needs is preferable to real life with a real woman.

Without looking too hard, we can find the same political, economic, and social concerns manifested in the programming of the major networks. Both *V* and *The Dukes of Hazard* were filled with latent political criticism. On the manifest or gross out level, *V* recounted in serial fashion the struggle of the human race to throw off an oppressive race of aliens determined to drain the earth dry of its resources and to use earth's population as a food supply. On a subtextual level, however, the military attire of aliens in *V* clearly established a connection between them and the same military-industrial complex criticized in *Short Circuit.* Moreover, whenever the aliens, who presented themselves as physically flawless humans, harmed a human, they justified their actions with the claim that what they did was for the good of the human race. The more intelligent humans, of course, reserved judgement and watched cautiously. Ultimately, we, along with the cautious characters in the program, discover that scaly carnivores lurk underneath the faultless complexions of the aliens and that the only way they will ever serve mankind is on a platter garnished with parsley. *V*'s warning was quite plain: be careful of whom you believe because governments and institutions are not beneath manipulating us for their own colossal and corporate ends.

By way of contrast, the *Dukes of Hazard* offers a light-hearted and comic look at politics. On the manifest or gross out level this television program recounted in serial fashion the picaresque adventures of the Duke family. Invariably the Dukes would find themselves forced to somehow outwit Boss Hogg and his corrupt sheriff, Roscoe P. Coaltrain, without circumventing the very law that these two villains would brazenly and regularly break. Although the manifest level of this program might be described as humorous or comic, the assumptions behind it were hardly funny. It assumed that government was corrupt, that a wealthy few owned banks, law, land, and industry, and that these wealthy few, though bumbling and ineffectual, were nearly clever enough to deprive the poor, benighted, and golden-hearted but average guy of his happiness, wealth, and constitutional rights. The subtextual messages of both the *Dukes of Hazard* and *V*, then, were the same. The large and powerful should not be trusted.

Airwolf and *Knight Rider* offer a deadly social commentary on the relationship of technology to the individual and to society. On the gross-out or manifest level, both programs recount the adventures of two knight-errants who operate on the periphery of the law. Both programs also contain the obligatory romantic interest; Stringfellow Hawk and Michael Knight must invariably rescue a damsel in distress. Both programs offer an element of obligatory male comradery; Michael, Devon, and Reginald of Knight Rider offer the viewer a father, older son, younger son triangle, while Stringfellow and Dominic Santinni of *Airwolf* offer the viewer a less complicated father and son relationship. Both programs also cast women in supporting roles, Bonnie in *Knight Rider* and Katlynn in *Airwolf,* and attempt to offer a token of appeasement to the young feminists in the audience.

But none of these characters and their relationships are essential because both programs, on a subtextual level, are panegyrics to technology. It makes little difference whether or not the main characters are sufficiently intelligent to operate their machines; all it takes to solve a problem, according to these two programs, is the right kind of hardware. Drug rings, international spies, and crooks of all sorts are captured because their adversaries, our good guys, employ superior technology and possess true moral fiber. The bottom line of both programs is simple: technology is inherently good and works always in favor of the good. We, the audience, then, find these two programs appealing because they reassure us not only that the good guys will catch the bad guys but because they also assure us that the daily onslaught of high technology will solve our problems in the future.

It takes little imagination to realize that the list of popular films and programs to which we can apply King's method of interpretation could go on and on. Indeed, the possibilities for reading between the lines seem endless. Of more consequence, perhaps, is the realization that works of popular culture, if they are to be understood and appreciated for what they are, should be subject to continuously critical reading and viewing—the very kind of reading and viewing that King advocates in his *Danse Macabre.* Consequently, it seems to me that King is far too modest in his discussion of the existence of the subtextual or the allegorical in horror fiction. He may well have been able to argue that the pleasing allegorical feel found in horror fiction is also found in many popular American movies, novels, and television programs and that works of popular culture often provide a quiet forum in which the viewers and readers of America symbolically address serious concerns of the day.

Works Cited

Booth-Bangor, Cathy and Kanfer Stefan. "King of Horror." *Time* 6 October 1986: 74-83.

Freud Sigmund. *The Basic Writings of Sigmund Freud* trans. Dr. A.A. Brill. New York: Random House Inc., 1938.

Gray, Paul. "Master of Post-Literate Prose," *Time* 30 August 1982: 87.

King, Stephen. *Stephen King's Danse Macabre*. New York: Berkley Books, 1981.

Ludlum, Robert. *The Bourne Identity*. New York: Richard Marek Publishers, 1980.

A Blind Date with Disaster: Adolescent Revolt in the Fiction of Stephen King

Tom Newhouse

Despite his reputation as master of modern horror fiction, Stephen King has consistently shown that he is more than simply heir to a set of stock literary devices invented by Radcliffe and Maturin and subsequently employed by most writers of horror and suspense fiction. Indeed, King does more than graft elements of a traditional Gothic formula onto a familiar modern setting: beneath their archetypal trappings, King's novels evoke the troubled atmosphere of contemporary America, one harried as much by the realities of corrupt government, technology run rampant, and an uncertain domestic life as by monsters and ghosts and other mythical products of the human imagination.

In contemplation of these grim social realities, King has devoted a substantial part of his work to dramatizing the problems of growing up within circumstances of increasing complexity. King's novels and stories that depict teenage life are profoundly critical of the parental expectations, conservative values, and peer pressures which teenagers must face. In addition, King's teen protagonists come into awareness engaging the contradictions between the logical realm of routine activity and the darker regions of violent, destructive impulses. They are often outsiders who turn to violence as a response to exclusionary social environments which deny them acceptance, or who resort to destructive attitudes that they believe will advance them upward.

King's earliest writings presented tortured adolescents and violence running amuck within the sterile, orderly environment of schools. "Cain Rose Up" (1968) dramatizes a college student's tense moments before he randomly shoots passersby from his dormitory window; "Here They Be Tygers" (1968) describes a young boy witnessing his tyrannical third grade teacher being devoured by a tiger, an unlikely occupant of the boys' bathroom; and *Sword in the Darkness*, an early unpublished novel, "is a lengthy tale of a race riot at an urban high school."[1] In addition to providing a context for displaying teenage confusion, the sudden disturbance of a seemingly stable social order anticipates King's special brand of fiction—a blend of social realism and archetypal horror, exposing deficient institutional and social values and the flimsy rational biases on which they are founded. While this assault on rationality is familiar to readers of horror fiction, King eschews the customary neutrality of social environment as it generally exists in most horror fiction. Rarely an active agent of evil in the traditional horror tale, King's flawed social environments are often directly responsible for the night-marish tragedies that proliferate in his works. King's fiction about the trials of adolescence, generally detailing a hostile social environment and value system, parallels his concerns with institutional irresponsibility that occur in his political thrillers like *The Dead Zone* (1979) and *Firestarter* (1980), or in his technological nightmares like *The Stand* (1978) and *The Mist* (1980).

Rage (1977) is King's first concrete expression of teen outrage and the first of the novels that he published pseudonymously as Richard Bachman. His most bizarre expression of teen revolt, this adolescent fantasy, remarkably, displays all of the familiar King trademarks: the colloquialism, the endless brand name references, the scatology, the perverse humor, the imaginative pacing of a tense but essentially static situation, and most importantly, the creation of a character type that would resurface in several future novels. Charlie Decker is the first in a long line of adolescent characters in King's fiction which includes Carrie White, Arnie Cunningham, Harold Lauder, and Todd Bowden. These sexually ambiguous, alienated, uniquely gifted, and destructive victim-victimizers are, despite their extreme actions, imbued with qualities, fears, and anxieties that seem typical of most modern teenagers.

In *Rage*, Charlie Decker, a student at Placerville High, fatally shoots two teachers and holds his classmates hostage. While not really a horror story, this psychological suspense thriller falls broadly within King's own definition of the horror tale. The action signifies an "outbreak of some Dionysian madness in an Apollonian existence"[2] that is analogous to the upsetting of the romantic, infinitely less complicated world that forms the setting of the Gothic novel. At the same time, King breaks with the horror formula by indicating a deep disenchantment with the arrogant assumptions of the accepted order. Charlie is something of a berserk teen philosopher, discrediting the notion that "life is logical, life is prosaic, life is sane."[3] Speculating on life's darker mysteries, Charlie gleefully muses:

The other side says that the universe has all the logic of a little kid in a Halloween cowboy suit with his guts and his trick-or-treat candy spread all over a mile of Interstate 95. This is the logic of napalm, paranoia, suitcase bombs carried by happy Arabs, random carcinoma. The logic eats itself. It says life grins as hysterically and irrationally as the penny you flick to see who buys lunch. (27)

But while Charlie, in his confused, murderous revolt, is a spokesman articulating the limitations of logic to make sense of the world, he is not beyond systematic, albeit perverse, calculation himself. Throughout the novel Charlie lays waste to all of his private and social demons by exposing the shallow tyrants of the established order and, in the process, shakes the foundations which they represent. School administrators and teachers are seen as hollow bullies, deluded by an authority that belies a weakness which is ultimately revealed during the tense confrontation, and parents are portrayed either as insensitive brutes or dark sexual monsters, like Charlie's Navy recruiter father.

Despite considerable distortion and stereotyping, however, King's point is clear: though Charlie's revolt has a basis in genuine madness, the causes of it are all too familiar and magnify the hostage students' similar anxieties. In fact, the day's unexpected events have a liberating effect on the students in terms of self-discovery and solidarity. If Charlie's classmates are at first repelled by the murders and understandably frightened by their hostage condition, most eventually lose the sense of danger and come to regard the experience as a valuable one. Some of the students even use their sudden freedom from artificial rules and constraints to make startling revelations of their most personal secrets, mostly having to do with parental misguidance, sexual frustration, and other sources of teen angst. Moreover, the students become quickly impatient with other students who spend the time challenging Charlie and questioning the compliance of their peers instead of engaging in purifying confessional soul-searching. As a result, Ted Jones, previously a popular student, is humiliated by his classmates, exposed as a duplicitous phony, and even physically beaten in a mass gesture intended to discredit Jones's deceptions (a trait which King clearly suggests Jones shares with his elders) and, conversely, to celebrate Charlie's and their own naked honesty.

The creation of *Carrie* (1975), King's first published novel, signals his substantial maturation as a writer.[4] While this novel deals with the familiar social milieu of cruel parents, a faceless high school, and painful rituals of conformity, King goes out of his way to achieve objectivity. A departure from the first-person confessional method of *Rage*, King employs a third-person narrator as well as the multiple points-of-view common to epistolary documentation, relating the unusual events of his tale through scientific reports, magazine articles, and a memoir. One positive result of this narrative method is a host of convincing characterizations. Administrators and teachers, previously clay pigeons for Charlie's gun blasts, are no longer defensively muttering empty platitudes. Rather, Rita Desjardins, the helpful gym teacher, and Mr. Morton, the assistant principal, are portrayed realistically, aware of the limitations of their authority and made more human by their failings. As Mr. Morton tries to remember Carrie after he is told of the shower incident, he laments, "After five years or so, they all tend to merge into one group face. You call them by their brothers' names. That type of thing. It's hard."[5]

Moreover, despite their being generally benevolent components in a system that, by its nature, engenders anonymity, the school authorities have the integrity to do the right thing in situations that require exercising fairness and responsible judgment. For instance, when the successful lawyer-father of Chris Hargensen comes to the school to legally pressure the administration to rescind punishment and permit the girls who abused Carrie to attend the prom, the principal defends Carrie and refuses to give in to his demands, even threatening to countersue.

The result of King's new objectivity is not only a meticulous realism but a shift in focus from the more abstract attack on the fragile nature of order and authority to larger problems of social organization. The primary agents of chaos here are Chris Hargensen, the snobby rich girl, upset that someone from Carrie's social caste can have an influence on her life, and Billy Nolan, the greasy, lower-class punk, who seek to punish Carrie after Mr. Hargensen's threats to the administration fail. It is especially revealing that as Chris wavers in her resolve to go through with the plot to humiliate Carrie at the prom by dousing her with pig's blood, it is Billy who insists, motivated more by a desire to assert dominance over his girlfriend, whom he resents for her superior social status, than by any hatred for Carrie. Thus, not only are clearly definable characters in verifiable relationships responsible for propelling the novel towards its end, but the final denouement has a basis in class conflict which, paradoxically, affects Carrie's fate both directly and indirectly.

While the conflict in *Carrie* is less generational than in *Rage*, King's novel is also significantly more disturbing than its predecessor because of its tragic inevitability. Despite the defense of the principal and the encouragement of Miss Desjardins and Sue Snell, Carrie's history of losing control and unleashing her dreadful powers, her impoverished home life, the demands of her religious fanatic mother, and the social realities that are so antagonistic, negate her unlikely moment of triumph at the prom with Tommy Ross. Because she is such a doomed victim, King makes Carrie's destruction of school and town seem more like an unconscious reaction than purposeful revenge, practically as impossible to prevent as the conditions which provoked it. Though not always compelling, King's narrative, with its labyrinth of explanations for the tragedy, underscores the problems of isolating simple causes based simply on personal vendetta and institutional incompetence, giving this novel a complexity and fatalistic ambivalence that his previous efforts do not display and that have little to do with horror fiction formulas.

The formidable destruction occurring at the conclusion of *Salem's Lot* (1977) and *The Shining* (1978) also proceed directly from realistic social breakdowns. The private moral corruption of the town of Salem and Jack Torrance's alcoholism and history of child abuse are tragic preconditions that fuel the developing violence made certain in these two novels by the further influence of supernatural forces. Not until *The Stand* does individual will prove to be a viable element of salvation, and even then it is only accomplished through a repudiation of old established values: at the conclusion of *The Stand*, Stu Redman and Fran Goldsmith retreat from the familiar codes of civilization that have come to represent the remodeled society of the Free Zone. Perhaps not surprisingly, then, King's next examination of adolescence presented the adolescent outsider not as some doomed victim of a damaged social order but as someone whose irresponsible exploration of the dark side leads to disaster. In *Christine* (1981), the only novel so far discussed that can properly be called supernatural, the outsider figure, Arnie Cunningham, is less the victim of the demoniac powers of the car than he is a half-willing participant in the dark pleasures which the fiendish car can offer, though parental mismanagement is still a factor in the direction he takes. Indeed, Regina Cunningham's rejection of her son's impulsive gesture to buy Christine, a broken-down wreck of an automobile, illustrates a reliance on overbearing rational control which, like most forms of limited idealism presented in King's novels, does little to prevent destruction.

And through it all she had continued to smile inside because it was all working out according to plan, was all working out the way she felt her own childhood should have. Their son had warm supportive parents who cared about him. Who would give him anything (within reason), who would gladly send him to the college of his choice (as long as it was a good one), thereby finishing the game/business/vocation of parenting with a flourish.[6]

But as the tragic circumstances indicate, schemes of moderation are inadequate to deal with the flexibilities and uncertainties of growing up. That some of these uncertainties are actually overcome as the darker side begins to taint Arnie's innocence represents King's most fascinating employment of his theme of teen struggle for expression in an unstable world. Christine's evil momentarily affects Arnie for the better: it gives him the nerve to call Leigh Cabot for a date, it makes him better looking, even clearing up his acne, and it gives him sexual powers he never dreamed of possessing. But Arnie's conscious participation in his metamorphosis blurs after his initial loss of innocence, largely as a result of his increasing resemblance to the car's previous owner, the evil Roland Le Bay, and corruption ultimately overwhelms him, making his short-lived transition from outsider to social participant, like Carrie White's, a kind of dream.

Yet without the active complicity of class conflict and an extremely debilitating homelife that makes Carrie's demise so imminent, moral responsibility can no longer be excluded as a viable element in the rite of passage separating childhood from adulthood. Unfortunately, this theme is not developed and Arnie is written out of the book in the final third, removed offstage by death with his mother in a traffic accident. Flawed structure and a shifting focus often characterize the works of popular authors who write as quickly and prolifically as King does. But in King's case, narrative problems like these are perhaps more emblematic of the tension that exists in his novels between social commentary and the exigencies of the popular storyteller's obligation to his audience. In *Christine*, it is the horror story that prevails. The metaphorical elements that Christine represents as an avenue to identity implicit in the mythology of the American automobile, given thrust by, among other things, the chapter references to classic rock 'n' roll songs celebrating the subcultural fetishism of cool, are reduced in favor of plot elements that must be resolved. Once Arnie is removed form the story, Christine's more intriguing functions disappear and she becomes merely a haunted car running down everyone in sight who even remotely suggests a threat to her, and who must be stopped.

Apt Pupil (1982), King's next exploration of adolescence, is a realistic story that repeats many of the themes of *Christine*—particularly the symbiotic relationship between good and evil—but eschews the tensions between message and genre. The relationship between good and evil exists in the fascination of a "total all-American kid"[7], Todd Bowden, for a former Nazi soldier, Kurt Dussander, who lives on the boy's street. If Kings' other treatments of adolescent trauma dramatized alienated teens trying but failing to conform to parental or peer standards, Todd Bowden suggests just the opposite. Unlike the others, suspended between conformity and revolt, growing soft in the battle and eventually succumbing to the tenets of the nightmare, Todd creates his own hell and is not subject to the gradual moral and physical disintegration of an Arnie Cunningham or the sudden destructive outbursts of Charlie Decker or Carrie White. Recognizing evil for what it is, Todd's revolt early in the novella against the hopeless mediocrity of his unsuspecting parents, consisting of a typically weak father and a not-so-typically deferential mother, and the stifling boredom of his Southern California surroundings comes as no surprise, and forecasts his evolution into mass killer. Though this novel, included as one of the stories in *Different Seasons* (1982), is ostensibly an attempt by King's publishers to show that he could write realistic fiction, *Apt Pupil* is scarcely a departure from King's usual obsession with horror and gore. Golden boy Todd is like a spoiled-kid version of Charlie Decker and takes King's adolescent oeuvre full circle by leaving the sunny California community strewn with bodies, the last of which is, interestingly, Todd's high school guidance counselor. Moreover, the intrusion of chaos emerging from a calm, seemingly orderly surface, exemplified here by "the perfect kid" and by a serene California landscape, is a theme that is interchangeable with, and central to, all of King's fictional creations regardless of classification.

Without abandoning literary archetypes and often imbuing them with metaphorical purposes characterizing modern life, Stephen King eschews the easy morality that much horror fiction promotes. By exploring various avenues of escape, acceptance, and social ascension, King dramatizes the complex journey that adolescents must make. With few exceptions, adolescence is a wasteland: no love, only sex—no family life, only an irrelevant and discordant existence that, as much through its shortcomings as by the confused teen revolt against it, is reduced to ashes. Ostensibly consumed for entertainment purposes, the fiction of Stephen King has special relevance to his readers by reflecting the emptiness of the post-Watergate 70's and the dread of the nuclear 80's, decades which historically parallel his rise as a notable contemporary writer.

Notes

[1]Douglas E. Winter, *Stephen King* (Washington: Starmont House, 1982), p. 28.

[2]Stephen King, *Danse Macabre* (London: MacDonald Future Publishers, 1981), p. 368.

[3]Stephen King, "Rage" in The *Bachman Books: Four Early Novels By Stephen King* (New York: Plume Books, 1985), p. 27.

[4]In his introduction to *The Bachman Books*, King indicates that "Rage" (originally entitled "Getting It On") was begun when he was a high school senior and completed in 1971.

[5]Stephen King, *Carrie* (New York: Signet, 1975), p. 19.

[6]Stephen King, *Christine* (New York: Signet, 1983), p. 216.

[7]Stephen King, *Different Seasons* (New York: the Viking Press, 1982), p. 105.

Freaks: The Grotesque as Metaphor in the Works of Stephen King

Vernon Hyles

The absence of tragedy in a tragic world, the lack of any absolutes, and the inability of man and the universe to mesh precludes tragedy and replaces it with the grotesque. Because of the ironic and absurdist bent of a twentieth century world that has seen all the implied horrors of Walpole, Shelley, and Stoker in living color and 3-D, the "thing that goes bump in the night" tale, popular and appealing though it still may be, has been misshaped and gnarled as Gothic conventions give way to other more modern tropes.

The horror story, the ghost story, the tales of the occult are all part of that eighteenth century Gothic tradition and are all viable forms in the twentieth century, but these conventions or tropes are creaky and decrepit from their two hundred plus years of use. They do, however, remain in the ghost stories of Peter Straub, the modern Gothic castles of Stephen King, and even the philosophical machinations of Charles Williams. What has happened, though, in our century, and this is supported by the definitions of the grotesque posited by John Ruskin, Victor Hugo, Wolfgang Kaiser, William Van O'Connor, Irvin Malin and others, is that the grotesque, once like Gothic a muchly used but misunderstood architectural term and the characteristic which makes up the soul of the Gothic tradition, has gradually displaced the sublime as a source of terror as evil is fixed in the consciousness of man himself, and he sees himself as meaningless in an absurd universe. When the forces of science, technology, and religion cannot destroy or control the grotesque—whether vampire, misshapen dwarf, or darkened subconscious—then conflict becomes futile and alienation and despair naturally follow.

Although major English writers of the twentieth century—Kingsley Amis, Collier, Golding, Virginia Woolf, Iris Murdoch—have treated the grotesque and used it as a major focus, it has been and continues to be a particularly American tradition. Beginning with Nathaniel West

56

and moving through William Styron, Truman Capote, Norman Mailer, Harlan Ellison, Thomas Pynchon, and John Barth, the novels of Stephen King culminate the continuing vitality of the Gothic. This strand begins with Brockden Brown and continues through Hawthorne, Melville, and Poe; it is present in Mark Twain (subdued in *Huck Finn* but dominant in the later short fiction); it is there in Stephen Crane and overpoweringly present in Faulkner and Flannery O'Connor.

To summarize this "new Gothicism," three conclusions can be reached:

1). The grotesque is the expression of the estranged or alienated world,; i.e., the familiar world is seen from a perspective which suddenly renders it strange, and this strangeness man be either comic or terrifying, or both.

2). The grotesque is a ploy against the absurd, in the sense that the grotesque artist plays—half laughingly, half-horrified, with the deep absurdities of existence.

3). The grotesque is an attempt to control and exorcise the demonic elements in the world.

It is obvious that, like all definitions, what has been said thus far about the grotesque seems to blur around the edges; in other words, "grotesque" does not have a constant meaning, but we may distinguish certain notions about it. First, the most consistently distinguished characteristic of the grotesque has been the fundamental element of disharmony, whether this is referred to as conflict, clash, mixture of the heterogeneous, or conflation of disparates. Second, critics on the grotesque have always tended to associate it with either the comic or the terrifying. Some have seen it as a sub-form of the comic and thus class the grotesque with burlesque and the vulgar. Others emphasize the terrifying quality of the grotesque and thus group it with the uncanny, the mysterious, and the supernatural. The tendency of modern critics, however, is to view the grotesque as essentially a mixture in some way or other of both the comic and the terrifying in a not readily solvable way. That special impact of the grotesque is obviously lacking if the conflict is resolved, if the book proves to be just funny or if what the reader had perceived to be comedy is in fact stark horror. The problematical nature of the grotesque conflict is important and helps to mark off the grotesque from other modes of literary discourse. But irony and paradox depend on the conflict of incompatibles, as do all theories of the comic which are based on incongruity or juxtaposition, but they are distinct, and the lack of resolution of the conflict is a distinguishing feature of the grotesque. Third, it has always been generally agreed that the grotesque is extravagant, that it has a marked element of exaggeration, of extremeness, about it, and this quality has often led to the association of the grotesque with the fantastic and fanciful. We generally think of fantastic as meaning simply a pronounced divergence from the normal and natural and so the grotesque is certainly fantastic; however, if we insist that the criterion be whether the material is presented in a fantastic, or realistic way, then we are more likely to conclude that, far from possessing an affinity with the fantastic, it is precisely the conviction that the grotesque world, however strange, is yet our world, real and immediate, which makes the grotesque so powerful. Conversely, if a literary work takes place in a fantasy world created by the author, with no pretensions to a connection with reality, the grotesque is almost out of the question, for within a closed fantasy world, anything is possible. Thus, a very interesting source of the grotesque is pinpointed: the disorienting and even frightening, but also potentially comic, confusion of the real with the unreal. Finally, the reaction to the grotesque—the experience of amusement and disgust, laughter and horror, mirth and revulsion, simultaneously—is a response to the highly abnormal. The situation where both the comic aspect of the abnormal and the disgusting aspect are felt equally is the focus of interest for the student of grotesque literature. The essentially abnormal nature of this literature, and the direct and often radical manner in which this abnormality is presented, is responsible perhaps more than anything else for the not infrequent condemnation both of the early Gothic and the modern grotesque as offensive and uncivilized, or as tasteless and gratuitous distortion or forced, meaningless exaggeration. Certain commonly used critical modes are in reality a part of the pervading form of the Gothic that we have labeled grotesque; for example, the modern use of "the absurd" in the context of literature brings it very close to the grotesque. Certainly the plays of Beckett, Pinter, and Ionesco fit our concept; in fact, we should probably be hard put to decide between "grotesque" and "absurd" to describe such characters as Nagg and Nell in *Endgame* or the orator in Ionesco's *The Chairs*. The formal means of presenting absurdity are many and varied: it can be expressed through irony, or through philosophic argument, or through the grotesque itself. Also, the difference between the bizarre and the grotesque is mainly one of degree, and the macabre and the grotesque frequently overlap; therefore, it seems that these two modes, the bizarre and the macabre, are simply sub-forms of the grotesque. There also tend to be interdependent relationships between irony, caricature, parody, and satire—all of which seem to be simply alternative methods of grotesque presentation.

Irving Malin calls the new Gothicism an exploration of "a world in which characters are distracted by private visions," and Richard Chase argues that the American novel is the current repository for the "profound poetry of disorder." Close to King, this new Gothicism believes in two things: first, the individual psyche is more important than the whole of society or politics, and second, the disorder and disintegration of the buried life must be charted. In order to do this, King employs a microcosm analogous to the old Gothic castle of Walpole and Stoker. The Overlook Hotel or a small town in Maine both suggest that a large panorama is not necessary to reveal that disorder is the primary situation of modern man's world. In these disordered worlds there is room enough for irrational and universal forces to explode.

Love, the most basic of those universal forces, becomes distorted in the modern gothic. King's typical hero, Jack Torrence for example, is a weakling who loves others only because he loves himself. It is an attempt to create order out of chaos and strength out of weakness, but instead it creates monstrosities. In the end, the only love that is viable in King's world is narcissistic love which is in itself disfiguring working symbolically much as Frankenstein does. Also crucial in King's concept of the grotesque is the family. It is used much as King uses the hotel in *The Shining* as a microcosm. What is shocking in this novel and in *Pet Sematary* is the process of familial disintegration. These three themes, the use of a small area as a microcosm, the perversion of love, and the disintegration of the self and the family, are primary in both King and in contemporary Gothic fiction. King's techniques also are those which have been selected by O'Connor, Hawkes, Purdy, and other modern Gothics. Order often breaks down; not only does the self and family dissolve but also chronology is confused, identity is blurred, sex is twisted, with the total effect becoming that of a nightmare. The use of dreams in King's stories and novels is pervasive; it gives to the entire canon that slight feeling of suffocation which strengthens the entire atmosphere. This dream-like quality is established in any number of ways, the most important being King's use of silence and darkness. In the modern Gothic tradition, if we are to have nightmares we must also have haunted houses, the haunted castle of the old Gothic convention, through which King's characters must pass into the other room.

In opposition to the haunted room is the journey motif. Characters like Jack Torrence and Louis Creed try to escape to the outside world or return to the haunted house, but whichever, all of these journeys end in failure; movement becomes as dangerous as remaining stationary. In dreams and on quests, especially in King's world, distorted reflections of the self are met. People have misshapen heads or bodies, they are seen only as silhouettes, or there are dark strangers who seem somehow familiar.

Like all of the "new American Gothics," O'Connor, Endora Welty, Carson McCullers, Paul Bowles, Capote, and so on, King's use of the grotesque, its tropes, conventions, and techniques, is pervasive; however, there can be posited two other significant influences on King's best work— his short stories, *The Shining*, and *Pet Sematary*. In *Danse Macabre*,

King's non-fictional analysis of the modern impulse toward the fantastic in general and the Gothic or horror story in particular, the author devotes two full chapters, fully one-third of the total text, to the modern American horror movie. King's prose can rightly be said to be a direct product of his love affair with the visual tale of the hook. As an art form, and here King defines art as any piece of fictional work from which an audience receives more than it gives, the horror movie at its best has the ability to form a liaison between our fantasy fears and our real fears. Reflected in King's prose, the same liaison is accomplished. Danny's fantasy fears are gradually replaced by our own universal fears—the fear of the father, the unknown, the dark, and especially the misshapen grotesque freak that, since Jekyll and Hyde, exists as each person's most feared doppleganger—in *The Shining*. Even more basic, Louis Creed's make-believe eventually becomes the reality of death, decay, the shroud, and the faceless, nameless undertaker in *Pet Sematary*. Horror films work for King in the same manner that King novels work for his audience. First, they frighten us by crossing certain taboo lines, or they serve as an accurate barometer of those things which trouble the night-thoughts of the whole society; for example, without the universal fear of death, a fear that each individual must deal with on a very personal level, horror movies and horror fiction would be in bad shape. The best King effects stem directly from what horror films have dwelt upon since the fifties, and this works mythically in that the Frankenstein myth, the "I am every dead thing" metaphor from Donne, and the Dracula myth of the inability to die, both are basic to our cultural and individual psyche. King refers to this effect as the fear of the bad death as opposed to the release offered by "good" deaths. Similarly, horror is derived from the decay that accompanies death. In a society that extols the commodities of youth, health, and beauty, all very fragile commodities, death and its accompanying decay and dissolution become inevitably horrible and inevitably taboo. The mystery of what lies behind the locked door is as basic as is the mystery of the mortuary, or what may occur in the local graveyard after the mourners have gone home.

I have included a list of what King considers the twenty scariest films ever made. Knowing King's fiction and being aware of his indebtedness to the conventions of the grotesque, there are several things which strike us as significant. First, in fourteen of the films, there is absolutely nothing *super*natural going on at all, and in a fifteenth, *Alien*, the supernatural elements are couched in science fiction paraphernalia. The conclusion must be that in order for a film or a story to be truly horrific, a strong dose of reality is necessary to get it rolling. The reader is propelled into *The Shining* or *Pet Sematary* or *Psycho* or *Wait Until Dark* by the feeling that, with the right set of circumstances, what is happening could well happen. The second thing that is evident is that one fourth of the films mentioned by King refer either to "night" or the "dark" in their titles. It goes without saying that the darkness provides the very basis for all our primordial fears. Even the films which do not evoke the darkness in the title do use that fear and rely heavily upon it for effect. Only eighteen minutes of John Carpenter's *Halloween* are set in the daylight, and all the major fright scenes in *Psycho* and *Looking for Mr. Goodbar* take place in the darkness with only the flickering strobelight effects used for illumination, and in *Alien* the constant motif of the darkness of space barely needs identification. Finally, many good horror films operate most powerfully on what King calls the "gross-out" level, a primitive, childish, let's watch Linda Blair spit out pea soup level, and many critics of King's work accuse him of failing to appreciate the characters they are watching as real people. If some artistic link has been formed, the audience witnessing the blood flying everywhere cannot remain unimpressed. Danny's final scene with his father in *The Shining*, with Jack Torrence because of the little bit of father left in him smashing that mallet time and time again into his misshapen, pulpy face, delivers the good gross-out wallop. And Gage Creed, or what once was Gage Creed, the little dead boy in *Pet Sematary*, slicing up old Jud with a scalpel comes too close to what King calls our common psychic pressure points. The artistic link is made in the best horror films and in *The Shining* and *Pet Sematary*, for we come to care for and identify with Danny and Jack Torrance and Hallorann and Louis and his dead son Gage and his reanimated cat Church and Louis's wife and her misshapen twin Zelda and Wendy. It is again that curious part of the grotesque where in bad horror the scene that is supposed to frighten becomes hilarious; conversely, the scene in George Romero's *Night of the Living Dead* where we have an old woman peering nearsightedly at a bug on a tree and then munching it up causes the mouth to try to laugh and scream at the same time, and that is King's and Romero's and the great horror film's remarkable achievement.

Before concluding, one last significant influence on King needs mentioning. Leslie Fiedler and King met in Boca Raton, Florida, at the fifth International Conference on the Fantastic in the Arts. I was fortunate to be a member of both a panel on Fiedler and on King at which each guest of honor was present. It was a curious meeting; on the one hand there was the young, hugely popular, writer of trashy, escape best-sellers while on the opposite side sat the irascible, iconoclastic literary critic. It is an influence that is either reflexive or at least osmotic in that, except for *Love and Death in the American Novel* which everyone of King's age and academic background read, the two men have travelled completely different roads. Being present at conversations between the two, it was evident that they were both cognizant of the similar ground they had traversed, and it was also evident that each felt a deep respect for the other. What Fiedler has done is to codify in mythical terms what King has done for the popular horror novel. In *Freaks: Myths and Images of the Secret Self,* Fiedler makes comments that could easily be applied to the best of King's fictions.

> The true Freak, however, stirs both supernatural terror and natural sympathy, since, unlike the fabulous monsters, he is one of us, the human child of human parents, however altered by forces we do not quite understand into something mythic and mysterious, as no mere cripple ever is. Passing either on the street, we may be simultaneously tempted to avert our eyes and to stare; but in the latter case we feel no threat to those desperately maintained boundaries on which any definition of sanity ultimately depends. Only the true freak challenges the conventional boundaries between male and female, sexed and sexless, animal and human, large and small, self and other, and consequently between reality and illusion, experience and fantasy, fact and myth.

Speaking of Todd Brownings' masterful film *Freaks,* Fiedler in the same book comments that its climax "makes explicit what Freak shows always implicitly suggest: that we only make believe that horror is make-believe." In the end, that is the power of Stephen King.

Sherwood Anderson called his preface to *Winesburg, Ohio* "The Book of the Grotesque." Clearly, Anderson was one of the first modern writers to purposefully become preoccupied with the frustrations that turn decent human beings into irrational, unpredictable, bizarre grotesques. West pictures a world in *Miss Lonelyhearts* that offers only disbelief, sterility, and emptiness. Nelson Algren peoples his novels and stories with morphine addicts, drunks, legless strongmen, and a central character named appropriately enough Frankie Machine. Paul Bowles has a character of his in *Let It Come Down* say that "today all of us are capable of monstrous acts which, even one hundred years ago, were almost beyond human contemplation." Eudora Welty's characters live in a land of dreams where everything is eerie, incongrous, comic in its grotesqueness. Carson McCullers's fiction is controlled by psychological motivation which is almost invariably abnormal or perverse, and Truman Capote's world is one where normality is presented monstrously. The supposedly nice people are really demented, and the young are wizened midgets, civilization is decayed, and things seem to be slowly running down. And always in the background lurks the man from Oxford, Mississippi, who gave us Addie Bundren's putrescent corpse slipping like a fish into the river, Ike Snopes's love affair with a cow, Benjy,

Miss Emily, and Joe Christmas. And there is Robert Penn Warren, James Purdy, John Hawkes, Flannery O'Connor, Tennessee Williams, John Barth, and Erskine Caldwell. And there is George Romero, John Carpenter, Leslie Fiedler, and Stephen King. What must be painfully obvious is that those creaky, decrepit old tropes—the castle, the love/hate relationships, the quest, and the supernatural—come together in the new Gothic impulse of what we have termed the grotesque. This new American Gothic replaces these conventions with new ingredients to satisfy the modern need for the bizarre, the macabre, the disharmonious. First, the gothic castle has become a microcosm which serves as the arena where universal forces collide. Second, the gothic castle functions as a means of imprisonment. Third, the gothic love/hate, male/female antitheses become, in the modern grotesque, an obsession with one's own problems, a turning inward to a form of narcissism. Finally, the modern grotesque takes the Gothic supernatural and shapes it or misshapes it into the something that is somehow all wrong, mad, or insane. The modern grotesque's supernatural is a geometry or at least a geometry that doesn't work, where perspective has gone crazy.

Much as the Gothic temperament was a pervading metaphor for the wild, romantic spirit of the late eighteenth and early nineteenth centuries, the grotesque has become the primary metaphor for the twentieth century world view and for Stephen King. Whether couched in the absurd, the macabre, the ironic, the comic, or the satiric, our grotesque condition, both as human beings and a universe, is the dominant outlook of film makers like George Romero and John Carpenter, literary critics like Leslie Fiedler and Irving Malin, and modern Gothics like Stephen King.

Viewing "The Body": King's Portrait of the Artist as Survivor

Leonard G. Heldreth

Steven King begins "The Body" with *"The most important things are the hardest things to say. . . .*Words shrink things that seem limitless when they were in your head to no more than living size when they're brought out. . . ."[1] Shaping important experiences into a form to be communicated is one of the major themes of the novella, and into it King incorporates several levels of archetypal experience. He cites the "high ritual to all fundamental events, the rites of passage, the magic corridor where the change happens" (p. 399); and even at the beginning of the walk down the railroad tracks, "bright and heliographing in the sun," Gordon Lachance knows he will never "forget that moment, no matter how old I get" (p. 328); as the adventure progresses, the hike turns "into what we had suspected it was all along: serious business" (p. 399). The journey the four boys take to find Ray Brower's body is more than just a walk along railroad tracks; extending through time as well as space, it integrates diverse rites of passage into one intensely concentrated experience.[2]

In the introduction to *Night Shift*, King asserts, "All our fears add up to one great fear. . . . We're afraid of the body under the sheet. It's our body."[3] Consciousness of the physical body—its sensations, vulnerability and ultimate termination—is the focus of horror literature; and while "The Body" is not a horror story, bodily sensations, the physical self, and the dangers that beset it are emphasized and analyzed. Starting over the GS&WM trestle high above Castle River, Gordon Lachance becomes "acutely aware of all the noises" inside him: "The steady thump of my heart, the bloodbeat in my ears like a drum being played with brushes, the creak of sinews like the strings of a violin" (p. 354). Halfway across, when he hears the approaching train, he describes for over a page how "all sensory input became intensified." Other descriptions of

64

intense physical sensations appear in passages describing the leech pond, the episode with the doe, and the beating Gordon receives from Ace Merrill and Fuzzy Bracowicz.

Beyond an awareness of the human body, a growing realization of its physical vulnerability draws the boys on the journey. The narrator's concern for such vulnerability appears in his comparison of Brower's body to "a ripped-open laundry bag," in his description of the dead boy's eyes filling with hail, and in his concern for the boy "so alone and so defenseless in the dark. ... If something wanted to eat on him, it would" (p. 383). Lachance went on the hike because of mortality, "the shadows that are always somewhere behind our eyes...what Bruce Springsteen calls the darkness on the edge of town" (p. 360). Going to view Brower's body is one way of acknowledging and defying death: "everyone wants to dare that darkness in spite of the jalopy bodies that some joker of a God gave us...not in *spite* of our jalopy bodies but *because* of them" (p. 360).

This desire to confront the darkness inherent in the body pulls the boys forward on what is, at the literal level, a journey to see death. The subtitle, "Fall from Innocence," refers not only to their loss of innocence but also to the fall of Man and the punishment of that fall by death. The boys' language indicates their awareness that this trip is more than just an overnight adventure. When Vern Tessio first announces the trip in the clubhouse and considers the consequences, he states, "This is worth it" (p. 294), and later he emphasizes, "we *hafta* see him...we *hafta*...but maybe it shouldn't be no good time" (p. 350). Gordon, speaking for the others, acknowledges, "the fascination of the thing drew us on.... We were all crazy to see that kid's body...we had come to believe we *deserved* to see it" (p. 391). What fascinates the boys at a level below their conscious thought is the archetype of the journey, whose significance they sense: "Unspoken—maybe it was too fundamental to be spoken—was the idea that this was a *big* thing" (p. 398). They never really question their "decision to walk down the tracks" (p. 397), for such a journey forward, in time and growth as well as in space, is as inevitable as boys growing into men.

This journey begins by moving them away from home and boyhood toward the world and adolescence. "Home...is a metaphysical principle and an ontological condition embodied in a place: the location which affirms who I am, projects what I may be, and vindicates whatever I have had to do to get there."[4] Abused or neglected by parents, each of the boys has been forced into a social identity which he despises; for each of the boys, home has become a limitation. Teddy fights against being labeled the son of a "looney" by Milo Pressman, Vern rejects being treated like a juvenile delinquent because of his brothers, Chris rejects his brothers and his father, and Gordon withdraws from his family that ignores him. Their small town environment has forced them into being "clearly defined contestants with titles, insignia, and traditional sexual or social roles," but they reject these roles, and part of their initial momentum, as they set out, "is the need to break away, or find a new home, identity, or commitment" (Elsbree, pp. 30, 36). When they are alone, Chris lectures Gordon on the need to go to college and escape: "I know what people think of my family in this town. I know what they think of me and what they expect....I want to go someplace where nobody knows me and I don't have any black marks against me before I start" (pp. 379-380). In the excerpts from Lachance's writings, Chico rejects his family and its lifestyle to head for Stud City while Lard Ass Hogan takes his revenge on his parents and small town society.

The movement of the journey to escape is contrasted with inertia, stagnation, and images of drowning. Chris warns Gordon to leave friends who will "drag you down.... They're like drowning guys that are holding onto your legs. You can't save them. You can only drown with them" (p. 380). Gordon equates this image of drowning with a life unrealized in two later instances: he dreams of the corpses of Vern and Teddy pulling down first Chris and then himself, and he comments about Chris, "I could not just leave him to sink or swim on his own. If he had drowned, that [best] part of me would have drowned with him, I think" (p. 431). Yet three of the boys do die without realizing their potentials.

The journey in contemporary literature tends to include "only the temporary lovers, friends, associates; more rarely the hard-won intimacy with a single companion, or two" (Elsbree, p. 42), and Gordon acknowledges that "Friends come in and out of your life like busboys in a restaurant...when I think of that dream, the corpses under the water pulling implacably at my legs, it seems right that it should be that way" (p. 429). In such a psychic journey, "the self is grateful to find it has the strength to escape the predation of others and to travel on alone" (Elsbree, pp. 48-49).

In addition to breaking out of a confining existence, Gordon tries to escape the domination of his dead brother together with the guilt he feels about Denny's death. Gordon has always been ignored by his parents and most of the town while they doted on his brother. Even George Dusset extols Denny's virtues and has "a beautiful vision" of the dead boy while he cheats Gordon at the scales. At Denny's graduation Gordon had rebelled and drunk too much cheap wine, but after the older brother's death the guilt returns, and Denny's ghost announces in dreams, *"It should have been you, Gordon"* (p. 309). The same guilt appears in Lachance's story when the corpse of Chico's brother Johnny returns with similar words. Brower's death, like Denny's, was accidental, and by walking to confront that illogical death—and thus his own and his brother's mortality—Lachance moves away from blind acceptance of the guilt and inferiority imposed on him by his parents and the town toward an acceptance of himself and the nature of existence: "Some people drown, that's all. It's not fair, but it happens" (p. 429).

Thus, while this expedition moves toward death in that the goal is a corpse, it also moves toward death in the sense of a journey forward in time toward the demise of the boys' own bodies. Dylan Thomas in the poem, "Twenty-Four Years," describes "a journey/By the light of the meat-eating sun" whose "final direction" is toward "the elementary town,"[5] and the boys are embarked on that same mortal trip. Brower's journey is over, as are those of the athletes who were crippled or killed, proving to Gordon they "were as much flesh and blood as I was" (p. 338). Dennis Lachance has also entered the "elementary town," as has his literary equivalent, Johnny May; and the beavers seen alongside the tracks will soon join them: "They'll shoot them some beavers and scare off the rest and then knock out their dam....Who cares about beavers?" (p. 391). Foreshadowings of the boys' own mortality appear all about them, e.g., in their flipping a "goocher" at the town dump (p. 337) and in Gosset's quoting the Bible to Gordon, " 'In the midst of life, we are in death.' Did you know that?" (p. 339). Teddy flirts with death in his truck-and train-dodging and nearly finds it when he falls from the top of the tree. Chico thinks, *"Nothing happened to Johnny that isn't going to happen to you, too, sooner or later"* (p. 310), and the adult Gordon finally recounts the later deaths of Teddy, Vern, and Chris.

Complementing these foreshadowings are images that confuse the quick and the dead to highlight the boys' inevitable deaths. After Chris falls down in the same position as Brower's body, Gordon looks "wildly at Chris's feet to make sure his sneakers were still on" (p. 415), and when Gordon tells the LeDio story, he sees the dead hero's face replaced by the imagined face of Ray Brower (p. 383). But Gordon's chief confusion is between himself and the corpse, for in confronting Ray Brower's death, he is facing his own. His dream of Denny concludes with the corpse's accusation, "It should have been you" (p. 309), but, so far as his parents are concerned, Gordon feels he is already dead. The "old reliable standby, 'Did your mother ever have any kids that lived?' " (p. 398) loses its humor when compared to Gordon's earlier remark about his mother's feelings after Denny's death: "Her only kid was dead and she had to do something to take her mind off it" (p. 304). The adult Lachance, looking back on his experiences at twelve, thinks "That boy was *me*....And the thought which follows, chilling me like a dash of cold water, is: *Which boy do you mean?*" (p. 419). The confusion is natural, for, like Margaret in Gerard Manley Hopkins' poem, "Spring and Fall: to a young child," it is himself he mourns for.[6]

Any realistic account of boys at the edge of adolescence inevitably involves sexual imagery, and "The Body" incorporates as one of its thematic strands the sexual preoccupations, ambiguities, and uncertainties of its pubescent heroes. The boys, all "close to being thirteen" (p. 291), reveal their sexual preoccupation in their language, whose most common expletive is "balls." For example, to describe fear, Vern says, " 'My balls crawled up so high I thought they was trine [sic] to get back home' " (p. 300), and Gordon describes fear as a polevaulter who "dug his pole all the way into my balls, it felt like, and ended up sitting astride my heart" (p. 354). Chris refuses to take a drink "even to show he had, you know, big balls" (325).

Sexual fears and insecurity are evident in the many references to injured testicles. When Gordon pulls Teddy off the fence around the town dump and they fall, the narrator complains, "He squashed my balls pretty good.... Nothing hurts like having your balls squashed" (p. 345). In the later fight with Ace Merrill and Fuzzy Bracowicz, Gordon receives a knee in the crotch and protects his "wounded balls," which Aunt Evvie Chalmers warns him "are going to swell up to the size of. Mason jars" (p. 426). Worse than injured testicles are lost testicles, a threat personified by Pressman's dog, Chopper: "every kid in Castle Rock squeezed his balls between his legs when Chopper's name was mentioned" (p. 336). According to rumor, Chopper has been taught to attack certain parts of the body, and an intruder into the town dump "would hear the dread cry: 'Chopper! Sic! Balls!' And that kid would be a soprano the rest of his life" (p. 333).[7]

The climax of this expedition is a test of masculinity in which a pistol that belongs to Chris's father decides the victory between younger boys trying to prove their masculinity and older ones trying to assert their power. A contest "where the testing and defense of self is central" (Elsbree, p. 133) is a common activity in adolescence, and such contests appear throughout "The Body": it opens with card games, climaxes with the fight over the body, and concludes with the boys trying to survive the game of life. The story also incorporates elements of the contest in other ways. Gordon's surname, Lachance, carries the connotation of a game, and his best memories of Denny, who was an All-Conference halfback, involve watching him play ball. In the embedded story, Lard Ass Hogan enrolls in the pie eating contest and, in his own way, wins.

The major contest, the fight over Ray Brower's body, sets older and younger brothers against each other. Both Chris and Vern are facing their actual brothers across the battle line, and it is Ace's mention of Denny that triggers Gordon's response: in insulting Ace he is striking back at all the people who have praised Denny and expected Gordon to be like him.

The contest in which the younger boys achieve a qualified victory echoes, perhaps ironically, epic engagements in the structure of its action and in its battle prize.[8] The corpse has no value except as an object with which to achieve honor or fame, and, as the story concludes, even that value is denied the participants. The two groups stand on opposite sides of a water-logged bog with Brower's body between them like the Greeks and Trojans on opposite sides of the river Scamander. First, insults and dares are exchanged; then minor warriors, Charlie Hogan and Billy Tessio, start forward, but are called back by Ace Merrill, their leader; Ace offers to negotiate with the other leader, Gordon Lachance; Gordon returns an insult and both sides prepare for battle. Then Chris, exhibiting his version of the armor of Achilles, fires the revolver and changes the odds. The phallic gun is particularly appropriate, as are the insults ("Bite my bag," "Suck my fat one"), for the conflict is one of masculine pride, and "Apart from words, the male often fights with the usual phallic extensions of self and/or weapons of power" (Elsbree, p. 26). Although Jackie Mudgett pulls out a knife, the more potent, adult weapon of the younger boys decides the battle, a victory anticipated by Gordon's earlier firing of the gun (sexual maturation) in the alley behind the Blue Point Diner: "'You did it, you did it! *Gordie did it!*' "

When the boys return home, Gordon, like the Greek heroes after battle, ritually cleans himself—"face, neck, pits, belly...crotch—my testicles in particular" (p. 423)—and throws the rag away. But the epic echoes and the masculine pride ("Biggest one in four counties") are all illusions; after the excitement of battle cools, Gordon acknowledges that Ray Brower's body is "a tatty prize to be fought over by two bunches of stupid hick kids" (p. 413). Such heroics have little merit beyond schoolboy conflicts, Lachance implies, because the outcome of any contest depends more on chance than ability, and the odds are against the individual: "they tell you to step right up and spin the Wheel of Fortune, and it spins so pretty and the guy steps on a pedal and it comes up double zeros, house number, everybody loses" (p. 378).[9]

A similar nonheroic attitude manifests itself in Lachance's ambiguous attitude toward sexuality. In the *Stud City* excerpt, Chico is a sensitive but typical car-crazy teenager with his libido in overdrive; the section opens with his deflowering a virgin and ends with his "rolling" on Route 41. But this early writing also describes sex as "Bozo the Clown bouncing around on a spring. How could a woman look at an erect penis without going off into mad gales of laughter?" (p. 312). The older Lachance describes the excerpt as "an extremely sexual story written by an extremely inexperienced young man" and as "the work of a young man every bit as insecure as he was inexperienced" (p. 322). The insecurity remains, however, in the comments of the older Lachance. It manifests itself in his feelings toward Chris, in his remarks about masturbation, in the leech episode, and in his literary allusions. When they separate after the hike, the twelve-year-old Gordon feels self-conscious about his love for Chris, acknowledging that "Speech destroys the functions of love" (pp. 422-423); later, as they study together every night through high school, he wonders if his former friends will think he went "faggot," but defends himself by saying, "it was only survival. We were clinging to each other in deep water" (p. 431). When he hears of Chris's death, he drives out of town and cries "for damn near half an hour" (p. 432), yet he cannot share his feelings, even with his wife, for such action would be considered feminine. Sexuality can be seen as hilarious but the rest of the macho creed remains locked in place: strong feelings must be expressed only in isolation or in a joking fashion.

Masturbation, another subject usually treated with humor, also has a serious side in the story. Jokes about it run through the story from Vern's "Fuck your hand, man" (p. 294), through the initial verdict on the swim and the parting speech of Gordon and Chris, to the last comment on the treehouse which "smelled like a shootoff in a haymow" (p. 429). But masturbation is also a part of the nostalgia for childhood innocence: for the boy "masturbation is freedom and omnipotence."[10] The adult Lachance associates the pleasure of his early writing with masturbation: "The act of writing itself is done in secret, like masturbation....For me, it always wants to be sex and always falls short—it's always that adolescent handjob in the bathroom with the door locked" (p. 360). Using masturbation as a metaphor for writing conveys the boy's and the adult's real attitudes better than the comments which the boys self-consciously swap among themselves.

The most disturbing sexual image in the story is the leech which attaches itself to Gordon's scrotum while he is swimming. When he discovers it, the leech is "a bruised purplish-red" and has "swelled to four times its normal size" (p. 393). When he pulls the leech loose, it bursts and "My own blood ran across my palm and inner wrist in a warm flood" (p. 394). As they leave, he looks back at the leech, "deflated...but still ominous" (p. 395). The image is of self-castration (pulling the leech loose) during tumescence and is more than a young man on the edge of adolescence can handle: he faints. The leech, a clinging third testicle, is swollen with blood like an erect penis (the opposite side of the image of Bozo the clown cited in *Stud City*), and both Chris and Gordon understand the inherent symbolism of the act. The deflation and the sexual significance, even for later years, are underlined by the adult Lachance's equating "the burst leech: dead, deflated...but still ominous" (p. 395) with the "used condums" floating off Staten Island. When his wife asks about the crescent-shaped scar left by the leech, he automatically lies, for even symbolic castration experiences are not subjects to be shared with wives.

This castration image, raised earlier in the Chopper rumors, is underscored by Lachance's references to Ralph Ellison's novel, *Invisible Man*. He equates himself with the protagonist for he is as invisible to his parents as Jack the Bear is to society. Gordon's dreams in the novella are negative—dreams of people pulling him down or of his dead brother's return—and *Invisible Man* concludes with a dream in which the narrator is castrated by Bledso and the others who have been running his life. They ask him, "How does it feel to be free of illusion?" and he replies, "Painful and empty."[11] Gordon also has been freeing himself of illusion: at the sound of the train's horn, his illusions fly apart letting him "know what both the heroes and cowards really heard when death flew at them" (p. 358); he finds he cannot trust George Dusset's arithmetic; and in the meeting with Chopper, he gets his "first lesson in the vast difference between myth and reality" (p. 342); he has few illusions about teachers after Chris's account of the stolen milk money; and he loses his illusions about death when he smells the decay and sees the beetle come out of Brower's mouth. The leeches lurking beneath the smooth surface of the pond complete the lesson about appearances: "The harder lesson to be learned is essentially paradoxical: how to live without illusion...and yet remain committed to some meaningful and coherent picture of things" (Elsbree, p. 41). For Lachance, the commitment is to writing: *"The only reason anyone writes stories is so they can understand the past and get ready for some future mortality..."* (p. 395). This statement echoes Ellison's statement at the end of *Invisible Man*: "So why do I write, torturing myself to put it down? Because in spite of myself I've learned some things" (p. 437).

Understanding the self requires understanding the past, and the story's final journey is Gordon Lachance's archetypal "return to a remembered place after years of absence" (Elsbree, p. 36). He returns in memory to the boys' journey down the railroad tracks, he fantasizes returning as an adult for the berry pail, and he describes an actual return to Castle Rock. Since the original events, he had "thought remarkably little about those two days in September, at least consciously. The associations the memories bring to the surface are as unpleasant as week-old river-corpses brought to the surface by cannonfire" (p. 397). But in recounting the associations he offers his "inner life, its genesis, changes, restlessness, and moods...a journey...through the growth of consciousness and self...and its interplay with the external world" (Elsbree, p. 42). At times he feels "like the pre-adolescent Gordon Lachance that once strode the earth, walking and talking and occasionally crawling on his belly like a reptile" (p. 419). He also identifies with the young man who wrote *Stud City*, "a Gordon Lachance younger than the one living and writing now...but not so young as the one who went with his friends that day" (pp. 322-323). The narrator, trying "to look through an IBM keyboard and see that time," can "almost feel the skinny, scabbed boy still buried in this advancing body" (pp. 338-339), for these and other stages in his development form a graph of personal identity, the self as "a construct or a series of constructs of subjective time which is inadequate to resist the march of chronological and historic time" (Elsbree, p. 46). In an interview, Ralph Ellison argues that the search for identity "is *the* American theme. The nature of our society is such that we are prevented from knowing who we are,"[12] and that the search for and unification of his identity should be a major theme of a writer as American as Stephen King is not surprising. The final (or current) identity achieved is defined in the last pages of the work: "I'm a writer now...and most of the time I'm happy" (p. 432), although in an interview with Douglas E. Winter, King reserves his right to switch identities: "I'm just trying on all of these hats" (Winter, p. 103).

Writing enables Lachance to come to terms with the emotions engendered by the adventure. The narrative exists in three reflexive forms—the basic story, the reprints of *Stud City*, and "The Revenge of Lard Ass Hogan"—the latter two being set in a different typeface. Within these forms are various narrators, from the twelve-year-old boy to the "best-selling novelist who is more apt to have his paper back contracts reviewed than his books" (p. 323). The parts of the narrative comment on each other. For example, the older Lachance evaluates the writing of his younger self, while the Hogan story begins as an oral account told by a twelve-year-old, switches to a published version written by the successful novelist, and then returns to the twelve-year-old's point of view. Later Chris warns Gordon that the pie story may "never get written down" (p. 378) after the reader has already read it printed, and he suggests that "Maybe you'll even write about us guys" (p. 376), the account of which the reader is holding.

Writing succeeds for Gordon because it offers control over experience. In writing *Stud City* he found "a kind of dreadful exhilaration in seeing things that had troubled me for years come out in a new form, *a form over which I had imposed control*" (p. 323). Writing and religion, *"The only two useful artforms"* (p. 395), permit a pattern to be imposed on the chaos of life: at the end of *Invisible Man* Ellison states, "the mind that has conceived a plan of living must never lose sight of the chaos against which that pattern was conceived" (p. 438). Writing permits a systematic formulation of the plan or world view and provides the means for keeping it before not only the author but all of his readers. As the narrator of *Invisible Man* asks at the end, "Who knows but that, on the lower frequencies, I speak for you?" (p. 439).

Most of the other themes of the work are incorporated through metaphors with writing. The body examined is not only Brower's but also the body of experience Gordon has shaped into the work and the body of works he has produced; the contest is the writer's attempt to decipher and communicate order out of raw experience; and sex appears in his analogy of writing to masturbation and artificial insemination. Writing, most of all, defines experience in relation to the narrator, a function he embodies in the metaphor of the blueberry pail which Ray Brower lost and which Lachance dreams of retrieving. He wants to "pull it out of time" and to read his own life in its rusty shine—"where I was, what I was doing, who I was loving, how I was getting along, where I was." Yet the act of writing has given him the blueberry bucket: through "The Body" he has retrieved the past, looked in its mirror, and found his "own face in whatever reflection might be left" (pp. 419-420). The words whose power he denies at the beginning of the narrative have enabled him to capture and communicate the experiences of his life.

To see Gordon Lachance as Stephen King is tempting. Many of the details match: the wife, three children, the million dollars from horror stories, the books made into movies, the youngest son who might be hydrocephalic,[13] even the luck (LaChance) which King acknowledges. Ray Brower's death by train and Gordon's close brush with it reflect the story King tells of an incident when he was four in which another child was killed by a train, although he states, "I have no memory of the incident at all; only of having been told about it some years after the fact."[14]

Concluding that Lachance is King would be tempting but unnecessary, for whether the writer is Lachance or King, an examination of a story or any cultural artifact returns us "to both the culture and the maker as individualized expressions of certain universal human capacities and experiences, of which the living through stories is paramount. It is this perspective which is so valuable—one which sees the human symbolizing process of story making as fundamental to culture, to our creation of an inhabitable world" (Elsbree, p. 132).

Stevens, King's namesake in "The Breathing Method," the next story in the collection which contains "The Body," says "Here, sir, there are *always* more tales" (p. 497); and indeed, as long as there are more lives, there *are* always more tales, for although each individual repeats basic archetypal patterns in his journey from life to death, his variations, like Kings' brand names, root him in his time and mark him of his place.

By translating these experiences into fiction, by sharing both the universalities and the particularities of existence, King and other writers help to break down the loneliness of life and even of death.

Notes

[1]In *Different Seasons* (New York: New American Library), p. 289.

[2]Douglas E. Winter discusses the motif of the journey in his *Stephen King: The Art of Darkness* (New York: New American Library, 1984), especially pp. 1-11.

[3]*Night Shift* (New York: New American Library, 1978), p. xvi.

[4]Langdon Elsbree, *The Rituals of Life: Patterns in Narratives* (Port Washington, NY: Kennikat Press, 1982), p. 39; I have cited extensively Elsbree's critical analysis of archetypes rather than the primary psychological texts because it carefully summarizes these patterns as they appear in literature and emphasizes the relationship of literature to life, exactly the relationship King and his narrator Lachance emphasize in the story.

[5]"Twenty-Four Years," ll. 4-10, in *The Poems of Dylan Thomas* (New York: New Directions, 1971), p. 143.

[6]*The Poems of Gerard Manley Hopkins*, 4th ed. (New York: Oxford University Press, 1967), pp. 88-89.

[7]Although the explicit sexual references do not seem as great in King's other works, a concern with testicular damage is not unique to "The Body"; see, for example, Louis Creed's need for "a steel jock" as protection against the deadfall and his dream of rescuing his son in *Pet Sematary* (Garden City, NY: Doubleday & Co, 1983), pp. 28, 247; Cujo's attack on Joe Camber in *Cujo* (New York: New American Library, 1981), p. 129; and the half-rotted branches that reach for Roland's *cojones* in *The Dark Tower: The Gunslinger* (West Kingston, RI: Donald M. Grant, 1984), p. 121.

[8] The narrative structure of "The Body" also resembles the epic in its embedding of stories within stories.

[9]King develops extensively this metaphor of the Wheel of Fortune in his novel, *The Dead Zone*.

[10]James Hillman, "Toward the Archetypal Model of the Masturbation Inhibition (1966)," *Loose Ends* (Irving, TX: Spring Publications, 1978), p. 120; Hillman's essay relates masturbation to fire-making and creation myths and sees it as having, for the creative inner life, "profound implications beyond a mere psychotherapy of the sexual function."

[11]Ralph Ellison, *Invisible Man* (New York: Random House, 1952), p. 430.

[12]"The Art of Fiction: An Interview," *Writers at Work: The Paris Review Interview* (New York: Viking Press, 1963), pp. 169-83; rpt. *Studies in Invisible Man*, ed. Ronald Gottesman (Columbus, OH: Charles E. Merrill, 1971), pp. 38-49.

[13]See the interview in Winter's book, p. 130; King also refers to hydrocephalus in *Pet Sematary*, pp. 270-272.

[14]*Danse Macabre* (New York: Everest House, 1981), p. 90.

Stephen King's Creation of Horror in *'Salem's Lot*: A Prolegomenon Towards a New Hermeneutic of the Gothic Novel

James E. Hicks

Most reviewers read Stephen King's *'Salem's Lot* as a tale of mysterious horror. One reviewer comments: "Those caught up in supernatural tales...will pore over every page" (*Booklist* 613). Another notes its "horrifying aura of evil" (Bodart *School Library Journal* 70-71). Remarking on the "ghastly, gruesome fate" in the novel, others review it as a "horror tale in which the sense of evil is almost palpable...." (*Publisher's Weekly* 208 109; 209 73). While these reviewers accurately describe *'Salem's Lot*, they contribute little towards its critical assessment, because they neglect to locate its position within the cannon of gothic fiction and fail to explain how it excites its readers' horror.

As Elizabeth MacAndrew points out in *The Gothic Tradition in Fiction*, the recent proliferation of gothic forms in television, film and popular literature demands a change in our study of this genre (241-42). In comparison to Mary Shelley's *Frankenstein* or Bram Stoker's *Dracula*, King seemingly erects a new hermeneutic of the gothic novel in *'Salem's Lot*. He creates horror, the "perception of something incredibly evil or morally repellent" (Thompson "Romanticism and the Gothic Tradition" 3), for his readers when he violates the American pastoral, constructs levels of intimate malevolence and establishes a cyclic pattern of childhood fantasy to adult reality in *'Salem's Lot*.

Unlike the European settings of *Frankenstein* or *Dracula*, the primary setting of *'Salem's Lot* is a Maine village with an emphasis on its people, their buildings and land: "The town is an accumulation of three parts which, in sum, are greater than the sections. The town is the people who live there, the buildings which they have erected to do den or do business in, and it is the land" (208). The villagers of 'salem's Lot, their dwellings and soil reflect the popular myth of the American pastoral.

As a native of Maine, King himself states that "there are so many small towns in Maine, towns which remain so isolated that almost anything could happen there. People could drop out of sight, disappear, perhaps even come back as the living dead" (cited in Winter *Stephen King* 41). The horror of *'Salem's Lot* is its readers' realization that the American pastoral is corruptible, that small town America is not a bulwark against depravity.

Refusing to adopt specific forms or conventions, the American pastoral is the unique expression of a pleasurable escape from urban sophistication. Like its classical and European counterparts, the American pastoral embraces the *locus amoenus* (the pleasant place), *otium* (freedom from excessive labor and the possibility for leisure) and Arcardia (the freshness of the New World in contrast to the decay of the Old World); unlike its antecedents, the American pastoral is realistic. Because America is real and the American pastoral is an immediate reality, there are few philosophizing shepherds in the American pastoral, though it paradoxically idealizes the American character and landscape. The American pastoral finds its fullest realization in popular images of small town America with its traditional values; however, the realism of *'Salem's Lot* shatters its readers' sense of the American pastoral and their idealization of small town America. *'Salem's Lot* quickens its readers' horror as it widens the gap between their notions of small town America and their perceptions of its incomprehensible evil.

When Ben Mears returns to 'salem's Lot as an adult, he sees the familiar landmarks of the village, revives a sense of his belonging to a particular place and recalls the security of his boyhood. Ben perceives the stable symbols of small town America:

He was amazed how little things had changed...the old tin sign pointing the way to the town dump was still there, and the road itself was still unpaved...and he could see Schoolyard Hill through the slash in the trees.... The Griffen farm was still there.... He wondered if they still bottled and sold their own milk. The logo had been a smiling cow under the brand name: "Sunshine Milk from the Griffen Farms!" He smiled. He had splashed a lot of that milk on his corn flakes at Aunt Cindy's house. (5)

The enduring commonplaces of small town America, its well-known landscape and its appearance of wholesome freshness, suggest the American pastoral, a belief in a less complicated life. While the readers grasp the implicit idea of the American pastoral with its ordinary images of signs, roads and farms, the horror of *'Salem's Lot* stems from its realistic exposure of small town America. As Douglas Winter points out, the "rustic charm" of 'salem's Lot is torn down "to expose dark truths" (*Stephen King* 42-43).

Similar to sprawling urban centers, 'salem's Lot exhibits the tensions of modern living, such as Hal Griffen's anti-intellectualism (34-35), Sandy McDougall's abusive parenting (38-39), Weasel Craig's alcoholism (42), Bonnie Sawyer's infidelity (59-60) and George Middler's sexual proclivity (211-12). With this awareness, readers realize that 'salem's Lot is not the *locus amoenus*; it is not the pleasant place in which to live. Hoping to escape from what Winter calls "the dehumanizing pall" of 'salem's Lot with its "art-fart" attitude towards the creative imagination (*Stephen King* 41), Susan Norton, a life-long resident of the village and an aspiring artist, tells Ben: "I'll be on that ten-thirty bus one of these days. Goodby, 'salem's Lot" (10). The natural setting of this Maine village offers little pleasure; there are few respites from labor or opportunities for meaningful leisure: "The land is granite-bodied and...farming it is a thankless, sweaty, miserable, crazy business" (208). 'Salem's Lot is not Arcadia; it is stultifying monotony: "There is no life here but the slow death of days...." (210). For the villagers of 'Salem's Lot, the vampire's kiss is almost a welcomed relief, since the wholesome facades of the American pastoral and small town America have collapsed under the weight of pervasive boredom and triumphant evil.

King destroys the American pastoral in *'Salem's Lot*. Like Norman Rockwell, he depicts small town America with its symbols of home, school and church; he presents the comforts of friendly companionship and family security; he captures the neighborliness of small town America. Yet he thrusts uncontrollable evil into the midst of Rockwellian America where Barlow drains life from the vitality of the American pastoral. It is not so much death which the readers of *'Salem's Lot* fear, but that death may not be final, that something can threaten their values from beyond the grave, that something so powerfully corrupt can rob them of their instinctual belief in myth as a source of truth. Realism is a poor substitute for intuition, but the realism of *'Salem's Lot* destroys the American pastoral.

Even though the violation of the American pastoral instills fear in the readers of *'Salem's Lot,* their horror is heightened through its levels of intimate malevolence, a hitherto unnoticed formula in some gothic novels. Levels of intimate malevolence begin with the death of a child, next an adult, then proceed closer to the protagonist (and readers) by the taking of a friend's life. The closest level of intimate malevolence involves a spouse's death. Using this formula, *'Salem's Lot* brings death and its terror to its readers through increasingly closer degrees of physical and personal intimacy. In this respect, *'Salem's Lot* resembles *Frankenstein* and *Dracula*.

Frankenstein is the prototype for the levels of intimate malevolence in the gothic novel. Violent deaths occur in a sequence which suggests a hierarchy of personal involvement. The four deaths in Shelley's novel indicate an ascending order of affiliation with Victor Frankenstein: 1) William, a child and Victor's younger brother (71); 2) Justine, an adult and family servant (89); 3) Henry Clerval, an adult and Victor's friend (176); and 4) Elizabeth, an adult and Victor's spouse (195). The assumption is that Victor would be less personally involved with William than Justine, Henry or Elizabeth respectively; nonetheless, the initial death of a child is important, for it reminds the readers of their own helplessness and inability to confront evil.

Like *Frankenstein*, *Dracula* exhibits a similar structure and exploits the same convention. In *Dracula* death first occurs at a considerable personal distance from Abraham Van Helsing's select circle, then slowly penetrates this intimate group. Three deaths take place in *Dracula*: 1) the anonymous child whom the Count has captured (44-45); 2) the child's mother whom the Count's wolves devour (45); and 3) Lucy Westenra, who is everybody's friend but especially the confidant of Mina Murray Harker (161). Stoker stops short of a spouse's death, but follows the same formula as Shelley. In *Dracula* death comes to a child, an adult and finally an adult friend: the child's death confirms the readers' powerlessness against wickedness, the mother's death signifies the vampire's willingness to destroy the family and Lucy's death establishes the domination of evil over virtue, three of the major themes in *'Salem's Lot*.

In comparison to *Frankenstein* and *Dracula*, *'Salem's Lot* shows a similar construction in its levels of intimate malevolence. Since Barlow's bite infects an entire village, the intimate levels of violence in *'Salem's Lot* exceed the formulaic conventions found in *Frankenstein* or *Dracula*. Like Shelley and Stoker, King structures an intimate hierarchy of violence in *'Salem's Lot*. Besides gossip, hatred and child abuse, he devises levels of intimate malevolence because Barlow's first victim is Win Purinton's dog (a pet), Ralphie Glick (a child), a series of friends (Dud Rogers, Mike Ryerson and Floyd Tibbets), a lover (Susan Norton) and spouses (the Glicks). King intensifies horror as Barlow strikes on increasingly intimate degrees of relationships.

'Salem's Lot exhibits a hierarchy of death, though it is unique in that an animal dies first instead of a child. At the lowest level of personal intimacy is Purinton's dog, Barlow's first victim as a sacrificial offering and portent of evil (40). Within the levels of malevolence in the novel, the pet, while loved, is the furthest from the realm of human interaction. The readers' horror is awakened at the senseless death of a dumb animal.

The first human death in *'Salem's Lot*, as in *Frankenstein* or *Dracula*, is a child. He is Ralphie Glick who, like Purinton's dog, becomes a sacrificial offering to the powers of darkness (73). The horror of Ralphie's death is emphasized through his innocence and name, which suggests his childishness and helplessness. Readers may be able to rationalize violence when it happens to adults; but when it is perpetrated upon a child, horror grows because a child is defenseless against evil. Ralphie's death underscores Barlow's malice.

The horror of *'Salem's Lot* is magnified for its readers when a large number of fellow villagers acquaintances, neighbors and friends, such as Dud Rogers (146), Mike Ryerson (165) or Floyd Tibbets (186), join the ranks of the undead. So many deaths occur in 'salem's Lot that it is impractical to cite them according to a strict time sequence. They are important, however, for they show the power of evil and demonstrate that the intimate bond among human beings cannot save their lives. Like Henry in *Frankenstein* or Lucy in *Dracula*, the villagers of 'salem's Lot find no help in friendship: Barlow perverts friendship and uses it to infect more and more of the villagers.

As in *Frankenstein*, the next most significant death in *'Salem's Lot* is that of Susan Norton (292). Like Elizabeth is to Victor, Susan is the closest person to Ben; unlike Elizabeth, Susan is not Ben's spouse, but their intimate relationship establishes the closeness of their bond (109-110). King seems to modernize the idea of marriage in contrast to its expression in *Frankenstein* or *Dracula*. In *'Salem's Lot* marriage, like friendship, is no safeguard against corruption. Marriage is another avenue which Barlow takes to work his evil.

Finally, the most intimate level of relationships in *'Salem's Lot*, like that in *Frankenstein* and *Dracula*, is between spouses. In *'Salem's Lot* husbands and wives fall victims to the vampire's bites and bloody kisses from their own family members, especially the Glicks. The destruction of the nuclear family is now complete. This excites the readers' horror, because the corruption of the family indicates that the vampire's evil lurks deep within the readers' subconscious. It is in effect the terror of ourselves; it is the fear that our hidden nature may emerge and take control, that family constraints will no longer be able to restrain us. It is, as Winter notes, the horror of our own identities (*Stephen King* 47-48). The horror of *'Salem's Lot*, like the horror of *Frankenstein* or *Dracula*, is the readers' fears that evil may take shape within the family and destroy it in the same way as corruption wastes the Frankenstein household, infects the Harker marriage or decimates the Glick home. Neither friends nor family can withstand the vampire's curse in *'Salem's Lot*.

In addition to the levels of malevolence, *'Salem's Lot* is similar in structure to *Frankenstein* and *Dracula*. Like *Frankenstein*, an epistolary novel framed by letters, *'Salem's Lot* is framed by a prologue and epilogue which enclose its narrative; like *Dracula*, also an epistolary novel, *'Salem's Lot* relies on the same mythology and includes epistolary documents to create literary suspense and to serve as evidence which lends reality to the novel (xiv-xvii; 412-23). Moreover, the prologue and epilogue affirm the circular nature of the novel. As a framing device, the prologue recalls Ben and Mark Petrie's flight from 'salem's Lot and the epilogue narrates their return; however, the narrative of the novel begins with Ben's homecoming and ends with his and Mark's escape. This ironic reversal of the functions of the prologue and epilogue is an important feature of *'Salem's Lot*, for it enhances and supports the cyclic pattern of childhood fantasy which is realized in adult reality.

In *'Salem's Lot* the worst childhood terrors of Susan Norton, Father Donald Callahan and Ben Mears come true in adult reality. Since evil is a hollow emptiness, as Saint Augustine repeatedly explains, *'Salem's Lot* contains a monument to malevolence, the vacant but seductive Marsten House, which becomes the focus of youthful fears and mature horrors. Unlike *Dracula* in which virtue conquers wickedness, *'Salem's Lot* refuses to allow goodness to triumph over evil and concretely demonstrates that the childish fears of Susan, Father Callahan and Ben become their adult horrors.

As a child, Susan heard the rumors about the Marsten House. She recalls her play associated with the dominate landmark of her village:

Amy Rawcliffe had a log playhouse in her back yard and they would lock themselves in and sit in the dark, scaring each other about the Marsten House, which gained its proper noun status for all time even before Hitler invaded Poland, and repeating their elders' stories with as many grisly embellishments as their minds could conceive. (27)

Susan's recollection is rich in its literary and critical associations. Her friend, Amy Rawcliffe, is a thinly disguised allusion to Ann Radcliffe, the gothic novelist. The reference to Hitler reflects Richard Wasson's interpretation of Stoker's vampire legend as a parable of Old Central Europe which seeks to destroy the New Western Europe and, by extension, America ("The Politics of *Dracula* 24-27). Even so, Susan, like Elizabeth or Lucy, is powerless to avoid her fate. Attempting to end Barlow's reign of horror, Susan is captured by Straker, Barlow's human familiar, and becomes one of the undead, thus turning her childhood imagination into an adult reality (292). Her childish fantasy in the log playhouse becomes a mature horror in the cellar of the Marsten House.

Like Susan, Father Callahan tries to combat Barlow's wickedness and fails. Father Callahan also possesses a childhood fantasy which is actualized in adult reality. He grasps the power of his boyish imagination when Barlow invades the Petries' home:

> Where had he seen that face before? And it came to him, in this moment of the most extreme terror he had ever known. It was the face of Mr. Flip, his own personal bogeyman, the thing that hid in the closet during the days and came out after his mother closed the bedroom door. (352)

Wanting to fight against pure evil, Father Callahan has his opportunity; however, unlike Van Helsing whose faith never falters, Father Callahan loses his belief and withdraws from his childhood fantasy, Mr. Flip, who becomes Barlow in adult reality. Once again, childish terror manifests itself in grown-up reality when Father Callahan is compelled by Barlow to suck his blood in a profane mockery of the Eucharist (355).

Similar to Susan and Father Callahan, Ben relives a childish terror in mature reality. In a ritual initiation Ben enters the Marsten House to retrieve an object to prove his worthiness. After picking up a paper weight, an appropriate symbol of the writer's imagination and the burden of the writing craft, he climbs the stairs which lead to Hubie Marsten's room, a journey that suggests an ascent into a conscious awareness of the creative imagination. Opening the door, Ben experiences his childhood terror which will later return in adulthood: "And there was Hubie, hanging from the beam with his body silhouetted against the light from the window.... And then he opened his eyes" (29). Ben relates that he is telling "the truth of what a nine-year-old boy saw and what the man remembers twenty-four years later..." (29). Ben's inability to explain his apparition in a *complete* sentence is noteworthy, because his experience remains incomplete. In order to complete the cyclic pattern of childish imagination to adult reality, Ben must relive his boyish fear as a mature grown-up; Ben's childish horror must reappear in mature experience. In *'Salem's Lot* horror is the realization of childhood terror in adult reality.

As a structural feature of the gothic novel, the circle or cyclic pattern has not yet received adequate critical attention. When Ben and Mark return to 'salem's Lot to disturb the vampires' unnatural sleep, they complete the cyclic pattern from childhood terror to adult horror. The circle from youth to maturity, from imagination to reality, from the unconscious to the conscious, is made whole. In *'Salem's Lot* the cyclic movement from childhood fantasy to mature reality is an artistic device which delineates character and reveals the darker side of human nature. It serves as a chart of the readers' deepest anxieties and fears; it maps out a geography of the unconscious. The readers' interior worlds are precarious and subject to pitfalls or even demons of their own creation; readers are horrified when they realize that their childish terrors are simply repressed by their adult minds:

> There is no group therapy or psychiatry or community social services for the child who must cope with the thing under the bed or in the cellar every night, the thing which leers and capers and threatens just beyond the point where vision will reach. The same lonely battle must be fought night after night and the only cure is the eventual ossification of the imaginary faculties, and this is called adulthood. (242-43)

'Salem's Lot makes its readers confront the darkness of their own imagination. *'Salem's Lot* forces its readers to examine their beliefs in myth, their anxieties over death and their insensitivities toward the creative impulses.

In *'Salem's Lot* King appears to construct a new hermeneutic of the gothic novel when he employs its time-honored conventions while using one mythology, that of the vampire, to corrupt another traditional belief, the wholesomeness of small town America. As the American pastoral withers, the readers discover that their ideals are meaningless: their friends and family disappear, their faith crumbles and their own deaths loom before them as terror comes closer to them through levels of intimate malevolence. The reader's childish imagination breaks through into adult awareness and they recognize the horror of *'Salem's Lot*: like a mirror, the novel reflects the readers' lack of mythology, their fears of the unknown and their mistrust of creativity. *'Salem's Lot* creates horror as it brings its readers face to face with themselves and they discover the horror of themselves.

Works Cited

Bodart, Joni. Rev. of *'Salem's Lot*, by Stephen King. *School Library Journal* 22 (December 1975): 70-71.

King, Stephen. *'Salem's Lot*. 1975; rpt. New York: NAL, 1976.

MacAndrew, Elizabeth. *The Gothic Tradition in Fiction*. New York: Columbia UP, 1979.

Rev. of *'Salem's Lot*, by Stephen King. *Booklist* 72 (1 January 1976): 613.

Rev. of *'Salem's Lot*, by Stephen King. *Publisher's Weekly* 208 (11 August 1975): 109-110.

Rev. of *'Salem's Lot*, by Stephen King. *Publisher's Weekly* 209 (7 June 1976): 73.

Shelley, Mary. *Frankenstein*. Ed. M.K. Joseph. Oxford: Oxford UP, 1985.

Stoker, Bram. *Dracula*. 1897; rpt. Oxford: Oxford UP, 1985.

Thompson, G.R. "Introduction: Romanticism and the Gothic Tradition." *The Gothic Imagination: Essays in Dark Romanticism*. Ed. G.R. Thompson. Pullman: Washington State UP, 1974. 1-10.

Wasson, Richard. "The Politics of *Dracula*." *English Literature in Transition (1880-1920)* 9 (1966): 24-27.

Winter, Douglas E. *Stephen King: The Art of Darkness*. New York: NAL, 1984.

Love and Death in the American Car:
Stephen King's Auto-Erotic Horror

Linda C. Badley

"America," writes John Jerome, "is a road epic; we have even developed a body of road art, *Huck Finn* to *The Grapes of Wrath* to *Easy Rider*, cutting loose a path to the dream" (Jerome 103). Stephen King's *Christine* (1983), a horror novel whose villain is only "an old car with pretensions," as reviewer Paul Steuwe puts it, is therefore pretty scary. It is a night journey version of that Great American Trip. It epitomizes a motif of automotive horror, one that emerges in King's first stories from the early seventies (collected in *Night Shift*, 1978), peaks in *Christine*, and extends to a more recent short story, "Mrs. Todd's Shortcut" (May 1984).[1]

One reason for this motif is that King excels at animation. Like Steven Spielberg—or Charles Dickens—he mixes mechanics and myth. Fritz Leiber, for instance, admires the way he brings machines to grotesque life (109-10). His automotive horror is just what the word means: self-motivating, moving on its own. His victims are driven, possessed, in a metaphor for dehumanization; whatever is in the driver's seat is not human. Hence King's monsters (whether eighteen-wheelers or lawnmowers) are horrifying for the rather obvious reason that they run over or away with you. Like the Frankenstein monster, once gotten going, they won't stop. "The Mangler" (1972), a homicidal Hadley-Watson Model 6 Speed Ironer and Folder (a demon-possessed industrial laundry machine), after "steaming and fuming over its sheets" (79) like a fussy dragon, finally wrenches itself out of its concrete foundations. Nor does it merely move off; at "an insane, blurred speed" (90), "belts and rollers and cogs...blend and merge, change, melt, transmute—" (91). At last, looming and leering, a "gaping, hungry mouth filled with steam" (91), it moves out to destroy the universe.

In running amok, the mangler joins a post-atomic techno-horror tradition in which automoting or moving down the road really means *going back*: devolution or reversion. It changes into an ugly American

Godzilla: no longer "precisely an ironer," it looks like "a dinosaur trying to escape a tar pit.... [Its] eyes filled with a great and cold hunger" (91). It means essentially the same thing as the gas-guzzling monsters of "Trucks" (1973): dehumanization. Vacant, moronically menacing windshields reflect a contemporary mechanization of human life in the metaphorical sense; they also announce the threat of literal extinction brought on by the fuel shortage of the early seventies. Like that crisis— and Hitchcock's *The Birds*—they just suddenly *are*: omnipresent, a universal "stench of petroleum" (141), omniscient, "headlights...pop-[ping] on in unison, bathing the lot in an eerie, depthless glare. Growling, they [cruise] back and forth.... The dark trailer boxes...like the hunched, squared-off shoulders of prehistoric giants" (130). The human race takes a quick time trip back to the caves, to "Drawing pictures in charcoal. This is the moon god. This is the tree. This is a Mack semi overwhelming a hunter." No, even further back than that, to a race of production-line zombies "in Detroit and Dearborn and Youngstown, and Mackinac" (142).

Along with the malevolent tank truck in Richard Matheson's "Duel" and Theodore Sturgeon's "Killdozer," King's automotive villains personify the external, corporate evil envisioned by the social and ecological consciences of the late sixties and seventies. But these hulking, stinking giants would not stand a chance against Christine, the monster for the "me" generation: the automobile. Christine is the all-American dream machine, a cornerstone on wheels. More importantly, the threat she represents is internal and domestic, involving the car as mobile home, womb, and image. The epigraph to Chapter 14, a song by Elvis Costello, makes the point: "about a couple / living in the U.S.A., /...they traded in their baby / for a Chevrolet: / Let's talk about the future now, / We've put the past away" ("Less than Zero" 117). Like *Cujo* (1983), *Christine* is about a threat to the family that comes from within it: in *Cujo*, man's best friend, the family dog, gone rabid; in *Christine*, the car. Moreover, Christine is the car become beast, the monster erupted from the Id during the glandular upheavals of adolescence. The institutional "Mangler" and the corporate "Trucks" were merely, if totally, destructive; the car has an intimately fatal attraction. In *Christine*, the *auto* becomes *erotic*. By page seven, Arnie Cunningham, Libertyville High's "Pizza-Face[d]" (150), four-eyed loser, has "fallen in love" with an equally passionate red and white 1958 Plymouth Fury, "one of the long ones with the big fins.'"*Let's go for a ride, big guy*, Christine seem[s] to whisper in the hot summer silence.... *Let's cruise*" (33).

If Christine lisps and vamps like an aging drag queen or a punk Marilyn Monroe, it is because, in terms of America's romance with the automobile, she is a bizarre national sex symbol—a kitschy grotesquerie that exists in a realm somewhere between the outrageous and the platitudinous, between the deadly serious and the bad pun, between myth and cliché. Names, brands, symbols *oversignify*: *Christine, Libertyville,* and *Plymouth Fury* compose an unholy trinity of god, country, and female principle. In an eternal triangle of boy, girl, and car, seen through King's glass darkly, she is the Anima as *femme fatale,* the Other Woman. As temptress, she offers Arnie, in fairy-tale succession, the charms of freedom, success, power, and love. These come in forms that a wimpy teenager can best appreciate: a mobile home away from his overprotective parents, a cure for acne, vengeance (hit and run style) on bullies with names like Buddy and Moochie, and a girl, Libertyville High's best looking one, Leigh Cabot. *Christine* is *Carrie* (1975) for boys: in place of that fractured Cinderella story (Yarbro), the revenge of the nerds. Like Mephistopheles, the car makes Arnie attractive but exacts a price: marriage until death, absolute fidelity—in short, his soul. It does not take Leigh long to learn that Arnie and Christine "were welded together in a disturbing parody of the act of love": that she (Leigh) does not *ride* in Christine; she is *"swallowed* in Christine." Kissing seems "a perversion worse than voyeurism or exhibitionism—...like making love inside the body of her rival" (196).

Christine is the Other woman at least partly because she is the Older woman, a junker to begin with, then a beautifully restored antique—though decidedly not a classic. Her sweeping, befinned chassis evokes the fantasy of a fifties golden age: a horizonless future projected in a perpetually expanding network of superhighways and an unlimited fuel supply. Christine seduces by recovering what seems like a pre-lapsarian vitality. Certainly whatever in her possesses Arnie is as primeval as the Mangler. It is a power representing the days when cars were big. One of her charms is her engine: her speedometer is "calibrated up to an...absurd 120 miles per hour. Had cars ever really gone that fast?" (15). But her real attraction has to do with her odometer, which runs backwards; "like magic" (303) or Rider Haggard's *She,* Christine regenerates parts, whether minor scratches encountered in the line of hit and run duty or major "trashings." Unlike the old car that sucks money "the way a vampire [sucks] blood" (17), Christine lustily devours time and soul. The version of immortality that she offers is a world of *Happy Days* reruns. Her radio, the voice of her soul, sticks on the Golden Oldies station—"The hard rhythmic sounds of Dale Hawkins doing 'Susie Q'—a voice from a dead age, full of somehow frightening vitality" (63). What Christine finally offers is eternal adolescence.

Fragments of some fifty rock and roll songs—about cars, love, and death—introduce each chapter: Richie Valens "screaming 'La Bamba' to a Latin beat," the voices of Buddy Holly and The Big Bopper (524).

Along with the songs (italicized as if slightly out of sync), she carries the baggage of a dead youth culture. Or perhaps *undead* is the better word. Evoking a folklore tradition of death cars in greenish, maggoty montage sequences, the stuff of two decades of drive-in horror movies, King populates Christine's back seat with reanimated corpses in various stages of decomposition and accompanied by the occasional waft of "rotting flesh and mouldering upholstery" (416). However seemingly unnatural, Christine's motivation is of the same essence as whatever has made Arnie's "glandular machinery...totally bananas" (says best friend Dennis, "I mean, [he] was pimple city" [2]). She is haunted by her first owner Roland LeBay, in life a loser whose "single-minded purpose," whose adamant "will," remains. A classic case of arrested development, LeBay possesses Arnie, who reverts, at first into a slightly tougher, older self (and to the horror of his conscientious vegetarian ex-hippie parents): a greaser, the "jd monster" that King has singled out as the prototype of fifties teenage werewolf moves, the "spectre" that "every parent trembled at," the "mythic teenaged hood leaning in the doorway of the candy store there in Our Town, his hair bejeweled with Vitalis..., a fresh zit at the corner of his mouth..." (*Danse Macabre* 52). At first an emanation of the raw, nervous energy of a simpler time, the juvenile delinquent reverts even further. In the following special effects sequence, Arnie's face becomes "twisted" and "sunken," with "only the nose thrust forward," into "some ancient carrion eater" (322)—into the primal self. Christine is a vehicle for its death wish on the world, for (in what becomes a kind of refrain, in italics and caps, and with pun very much intended) an "everlasting Fury" unleashed on "SHITTERS": car trashers, s.o.b.'s, whoever or whatever gets in the way.

Christine is therefore, after all, only the vehicle: she functions as Arnie's double, but it is LeBay's alienation that has made her the bitch that she is. King's real monster is the partly domesticated male, the territorial Id or embryonic anti-hero. The aggression that the death car effects against Arnie's male antagonists has its other side in sexual impotence, lovelessness, fetishism. Counterpointing the refrain about "SHITTERS" is LeBay's favorite joke about the "smell of a brand-new car": it is " 'about the finest smell in the world.' [LeBay] considered. 'Except maybe for pussy' " (10). Roland "was not a good man," explains his brother George. "I believe the only thing he ever truly loved in his whole life was that Plymouth Fury" (91). LeBay's indifference—or, at the very most, only secondary interest—in the feminine extends to his family in acts of passive aggression. LeBay once looked away as his daughter strangled to death and his wife committed suicide. Arnie reenacts these episodes as Leigh chokes on a McDonald's hamburger; he fails to remember the Heimlich Maneuver. "The Life You Save My Be Your

Own," warned Flannery O'Connor in a similar parable of automotive egotism in 1957, in which a Mr. Shiftlet abandons his retarded deaf-mute bride at a roadside diner and drives on to (where else?) Mobile. Consider "the cars we zip ourselves up in, thereby becoming anonymous...and perhaps homicidal," says King in *Danse Macabre*, and you will experience a feeling of "deep, almost primitive unease" (162).

"Love is not blind. Love is a cannibal with extremely acute vision. Love is insecticide; it is always hungry," explains George LeBay to Dennis Guilder, Arnie's best friend. "What does it eat?... Friendship" (91). The Plymouth Fury is the love that kills. Christine's watchful, jealous devotion (she has a greeneyed dashboard) not only comes between Arnie and Leigh, but also destroys the archetypal buddy system represented in All-American Dennis and Arnie-the-sidekick. It is no oversight on King's part that *Christine* is almost pristine, as far as explicit or hetero sex is concerned. As Arnie regresses, Dennis sees that "The mouth [has] taken all the tucks of sour loneliness. Because this...thing, apparition, whatever it was—it was alone.... Alone except for Christine" (322). The car is an animistic projection of his infantile narcissism, his auto-eroticism.

The novel is therefore a characteristic example of what Irving Malin has called *New American Gothic* (1962), whose subtext and real horror is withdrawal, a turning inward, the self one-to-one on itself. As Christopher Lasch argues in *The Culture of Narcissism: American Life in an Age of Diminishing Expectations* (1979), this cultural neurosis has culminated in the "me" generation that began in the late seventies and continues into the eighties. *Christine* suggests, moreover, that the sociopathic juvenile is the double of the narcissistic nerd who whimpered his way through songs like "Teen Angel," "Dream Lover," and "In My Room." In the same way, the "heavy metal" image that Christine suggests had its softer, introverted double in television shows like the infantile *Love Bug* or the Oedipal *My Mother, The Car*.

No simple killing machine, Christine is a womb on wheels, a dark cocoon of sound. In a novel of some five hundred pages, Arnie actually travels to a football game, does a little Christmas shopping, and grabs the requisite Big Mac. Most of the trips taken in Christine are in or out of time: a dim recollection of a "gunn[ing] and f[alling] off, gunn[ing] and f[alling] off. Faintly, like something from a lunatic's nightmare,...Elvis Presley singing 'Jailhouse Rock' " (289). Dream lovers, at least automotive ones, have a way of turning into nightmares; Christine takes Arnie nowhere but the twilight zone. It is the driver's *seat* that provides the illusion of freedom, of the power of autogenesis. "The spirit," moralizes O'Connor's Shiftlet, "is like a automobile: always on the move, always" (166). Similarly Steve Kemp, *Cujo*'s occasional poet and full-time American Adam (Lewis), after vandalizing his lover's suburban home, drives west toward "country that sprawled...to the silent reaches of Idaho" where "Papa Hemingway had gone to when...mortally hurt." He feels the "familiar lift" that comes with "cutting old ties": then "newborn," he comes into "possession of the greatest freedom of all, the freedom to recreate himself" (211). He takes the prototypical journey of adolescence and of America—the journey of Huck "lighting out for the territory"*(Cujo* 211), transcending civilization and history. *Christine* recapitulates that journey fifties style—in the form of a fatal nostalgia trip.

As Douglas Winter has suggested, the novel is in part a "dark parable about the death of the American romance with the automobile," one that "enacts" its "last gasp" (125) or final backfire. Indeed, if *Christine* appears to focus on adolescence, the subtext is America's coming of age from the opposite end. Written by a now-fortyish King and set in the not quite eighties, it diagnoses a cultural midlife crisis. It is in keeping with such a mood or time of life that King chose the 1958 Plymouth Fury: not so much for its name as for its absolute mediocrity, its typicality. "That car summed up the fifties," King said in a 1984 interview: "it was a very bland, ordinary, mass-produced car" (Winter 124). It is also in keeping with such a mood that King cultivates his peculiar deadpan style of camp, the archetypal method that is not quite myth and not quite cliché, the deliberately awful humor that moves somewhere between titillation and parody. On one level, *Christine* is as American as apple pie, as pure as the Mayflower, and more comforting than Mom. The nostalgia appeals on the level of *Leave It to Beaver* reruns; the family conflicts are the stuff of fifties TV sitcoms. Arnie is named after "Arnold's" and Richie Cunningham, the local hangout and lead character of *Happy Days*, the nostalgic seventies television series set in the fifties (Winter 124). On the other hand, this coyness in the style of *American Graffiti* or *Grease* is shown to be decadent, even sinister, as Christine herself is sinister. King seems to have cultivated a peculiar *deja vu* effect which evokes nostalgia and simultaneously makes a point about it. During their last ride together, Dennis and Arnie

went back in time, but did we? The present-day streets of Libertyville were still there, but they were like a thin overlay of film...as if...the late 1970s had been drawn on Saran Wrap and laid over a time that was somehow more real, and I could feel that time reaching its dead hands out toward us, trying to catch us and draw us in for ever.... The cars parked along the street...all seemed to be pre-60s.... Long portholed Buicks.... Packards, bullet-nosed Studebakers, and once, fantastical and new, an Edsel.

'Yeah, this year is going to be better,' Arnie [said, raising] his beer-can to his lips and before it got there his face had turned to LeBay's, a rotting figure from a horror comic. (417)

This passage is doubly interesting for describing the perspective of the novel as a whole: the late seventies superimposed on a stylized representation of the fifties—on a concept, created in retrospect, of an original car and youth culture. Paul Steuwe, who is evidently, like King, a baby boomer, suggests that "it's as if we're dealing with our callow former selves...." The effect is enhanced by point of view; *Christine* is narrated in part by an older, deracinated Dennis Guilder who perceives himself, even while projecting back into the time in which the story is set, in terms of a prototype from the fifties. If he finds the teenagers in the movie *Grease*, which his cheerleader girlfriend loves, "dumb" and "totally unreal," but in contrast to those in "authentic" fifties movies: "(if I want realistic teenagers...I'll catch *The Blackboard Jungle* sometime on a revival)..." (80). For this late seventies adolescent, a "teenager" is not a group with which he identifies directly but a fifties type, a film image, and an icon.

This perspective suggests that *Christine* is for as well as about teenagers who perceive their identities in relation to the icons of the late fifties, *American Graffiti* style. Like *Grease*, *Christine* is a recapitulatory rock musical. Plot and theme correspond with the fifty-odd songs from 1956 through 1983. These are arranged in Leslie Fiedler's terms in *Love and Death in the American Novel*—"Teenage Car Songs," "Teenage Love Songs," and "Teenage Death Songs"—with the "car" category subsuming the other two. It all adds up to a bid for the Great Adolescent American Horror Novel, one in which "Teen Angel" meets "Maybelline" and "Mary Lou," and "Little Deuce Coupe" drags "Buick 59" on "Dead Man's Curve."

What kind of nostalgia is this? When taking the shapes of LeBay and Christine it is shown to be ghoulish. When seen as informing the perspective and the appeal of the novel itself, it becomes more problematic. Like *Creepshow*'s deliberate throwback to E.C. Comics, *Christine* distances and then familiarizes both the terror and the past by camping it up: setting it in a comic strip bubble and freeze-framing it, making it safe, even cosy. Watching the filming of "The Crate," Ron Hansen writes, "You're minutes ahead of the characters, aware of every switchback and twist...even some of the crew members smile; the filmmakers [King and George Romero] have not missed a trick" (72). The perspective of *Christine* is similar in being deliberately predictable, like a re-enactment. Paul Gray views the formal issue in terms of what he calls "postliterate prose," which by "plugging directly into pre-fabricated images," by using language to "remind [readers] of what they have already seen" (much as music videos remind viewers of what they have already heard), appeals "to people who do not ordinarily like to read," who would rather have their preconceptions reinforced. Of course, none of this should bother King, whose foreword to a collection of critical essays on his fiction is called "On Becoming a Brand Name." And it is no surprise to see, on the first page of a recent Sunday newspaper advertising section for area Target stores, between the Memorex video tapes and store brand elastic leg diapers, a two-for-five-dollar sale on King paperbacks ("Target Sale").

The perfect form for our protracted American adolescence, *Christine* is a symptom of the cultural phenomenon it examines: a new species of anachronism or *deja vu* that disguises its real nature as a narcissistic reaction to future shock. The late seventies and the fifties blur together: a Saran Wrap window frames, in an illusion of seamless permanence, the past and the present, and the horrifying side of which is the prospect of living an infinite replay. *Christine* is about a cultural midlife crisis that re-enacts adolescence; it is also about adolescence as a self-perpetuating cycle. The novel reflects not one but at least two generations of middle-aged adolescents. One is King's age and is reliving the past; the other, younger, but more self-consciously "punk" generation consists of rebels without causes who have too many vehicles, who are all dressed up, with no place to go. In so doing , it suggests an intimate relationship between the timeless (or is it haunted?) world of adolescence and our contemporary American way of life. In Dennis's nightmares, years after the events of the main story have taken place, Christine appears wearing a vanity plate, a "grinning white skull on a dead black field" and imprinted with the words," 'ROCK 'N' ROLL WILL NEVER DIE' " (502).

Christine makes yet another return appearance in May of 1984 in *Redbook*—and as adult fantasy. In "Mrs. Todd's Shortcut," labeled on the cover a "CHILLER," she's a '64 or '65 champagne-colored "two-seater sportster" (58), a decidedly masculine Mercedes "go-devil" whose engine idles "heavy, the way the old ones do that still run full bore straight ahead and damn the torpedoes. Now that I think of it, that car *looked* like a torpedo" (188). As *Christine* is at least superficially for and about teens, this story concerns midlife crisis. It is directed specifically toward ladies of a certain age. The car, whose odometer works a lot like Christine's, becomes a means of transcendence for Ophelia Todd, the total woman's notion of an alienated loser: "Worth Todd's wife who could never carry a child to term" and "who tried to write poetry and failed at it…" (188). What she succeeds in is the shortcut.

As in *Christine*, going forward really means going backwards; what seems like extroversion is revealed as obsession and narcissistic fantasy. At the beginning of the tale, portrayed as a creator of spots of quality time, Mrs. Todd becomes obsessed with beating the clock—and does. Time, or, rather, control of it—"*knowing* how to get there quick"— "that has power" (178), she explains. She grows younger until, about sixteen, she is "like that woman drivin' the moon across the sky,...with her gossamer stoles all flyin' out behind her in silver cobwebs and her hair streamin' back..., lashen' those horses and tellin' 'em... faster, *faster*" (181). She becomes Diana or the White Goddess. "Moon was her go-devil" (182). Taking with her a local yokel named Homer Buckland, a New England version of Wandering Aengus or "The Man Who dreamed of Faeryland," she disappears—and not into the twilight zone or a fifties "Rock Around the Clock" but into the Celtic Twilight: a land of creepy crawlies, "wavin' grasses," "plants that make faces," and "somethin settin' in a squat on top of a stump..." (182). When last seen, "Gorgeous and wild and...untamed" (186) she radiates a "terrible" beauty that makes the narrator's heart drop dead at her feet (188).

The romance ends mysteriously, in an ambiguity that can suggest a sort of apotheosis. Mrs. Todd becomes a local legend, Great American Bitch transformed into one of Yeats' glimmering girls. Her shortcut is to immortality. But then, as we learn in the fifth paragraph, folks are "still not done talking about Joe Camber, who got killed by his own dog" (56); her immortality is of the same evil substance as Cujo's. Perhaps the shortcut refers to the chill that undercuts the romance or the disturbing abruptness of the "vanishing," whose sardonically evil humor is akin to the mood in which Lewis Carroll concluded *The Hunting of the Snark*. Is "Mrs. Todd's Shortcut," in other words, another *Christine*, as the name Ophelia Todd overwhelmingly suggests? Does it end in a void and another triumph of the Death Car, in a replay? As Mrs. Todd explains, "All a woman wants is what a man wants—a woman wants to *drive*" (188).

Recent popular songs like "She Loves My Car" (Ronnie Milsap) or "She Don't Love Me, She Loves My Automobile" (Leon Redbone), suggest with Mrs. Todd that the women's movement has not changed the picture, really; it has merely reversed the roles. Women now share Arnie Cunningham's susceptibility to auto-neurosis. Perhaps the disease is, after all, existential. It is significant that the one epigraph in *Christine* that is not from a popular song is a poem by Robert Creeley, quoted in its entirety except for the title, "I Know a Man" (466). In it the speaker, who characterizes himself as "always talking," experiences a glimmering recognition of the absurd, of the awful fact that "darkness sur- / rounds us." "[W]hat can we do against it[?]" he then asks. His answer is simple

and all-American: "shall we & / why not, buy a goddamn big car...."
(466).

Notes

[1]After this article was written, "Mrs. Todd's Shortcut" was collected in *Skeleton Crew* (1985), Scream Press and Putnam; 1986, Signet-NAL), and "Trucks" was adapted to film in *Maximum Overdrive*, directed by King and produced by Dino de Laurentiis (North Carolina Film Corporation, 1985).

Works Cited

Dettelbach, Cynthia. *In the Driver's Seat: The Automobile in American Literature and Popular Culture.* Contributions in American Studies, 25. Westport and London: Greenwood, 1976.

Fiedler, Leslie. *Love and Death in the American Novel.* New York: Criterion, 1960.

Gray, Paul. "Master of Postliterate Prose." *Time* 120 (30 Aug. 1982): 87.

Hansen, Ron. "*Creepshow*: The Dawn of a Living Horror Comedy." *Esquire* 97 (Jan. 1982): 72-73, 76.

Jerome, John. *The Death of the Automobile: The Fatal Effect of the Golden Era, 1955-1970.* New York: Norton, 1972.

King, Stephen, *Carrie.* Garden City: Doubleday, 1974.

——— *Christine.* 1983. New York: Signet-NAL, 1984.

——— screenwriter. *Creepshow.* Dir. George Romero. Warner Brothers, 1982.

——— *Cujo.* New York: Viking, 1981.

——— *Danse Macabre.* 1981. New York: Berkley, 1982.

——— "The Mangler." King, *Night Shift* 74-92.

——— "Mrs. Todd's Shortcut." *Redbook* May 1984: 56, 58, 178, 181-82, 184, 185-88.

——— *Night Shift.* 1978. New York: Signet-NAL, 1979.

——— "On Becoming a Brand Name." Foreword. Underwood and Miller 15-42.

——— *The Shining.* Garden City: Doubleday, 1977.

——— "Trucks," King, *Night Shift* 127-42.

Lasch, Christopher. *The Culture of Narcissism: American Life in an Age of Diminishing Expectations.* New York: Warner, 1979.

Lewis, R.W.B. *The American Adam.* Chicago: Chicago UP, 1955.

Leiber, Fritz. "Horror Hits a High." Underwood and Miller 103-121.

Malin, Irving. *The New American Gothic.* Crosscurrents Modern Critiques. Carbondale: Southern Illinois UP, 1962.

O'Connor, Flannery. "The Life You Save May Be Your Own." *A Good Man is Hard to Find.* 1955. *3 by Flannery O'Connor.* New York: Signet-NAL, 1962. 161-70.

Stuewe, Paul. Rev. of *Christine.* By Stephen King. *Quill Quire* 49 (June 1983): 37.

"Target Sale." Newspaper Advertising Supplement. *The Tennessean* [Nashville] 30 Sept. 1984.

Underwood, Tim, and Chuck Miller, ed. *Fear Itself: The Horror Fiction of Stephen King*. New York: Signet-NAL, 1984.

Winter, Douglas. *Stephen King: The Art of Darkness*. New York: NAL, 1984.

Yarbro, Chelsea Quinn. "Cinderella's Revenge: Twists on Fairy Tale and Mythic Themes in the Work of Stephen King." Underwood and Miller 63-74.

The Dark Tower:
Stephen King's Gothic Western

James Egan

Stephen King's *The Dark Tower* first appeared as five short stories, each with a separate title, between October of 1978 and November of 1981. The stories were collected as *The Dark Tower: The Gunslinger* and published in limited editions of ten thousand copies in October of 1982 and April of 1984. Though King concedes that the novel could easily be expanded,[1] the episodes in print are complete and fully unified, roughly equivalent to one self-contained stanza of a poem. He has established the structural, generic and thematic framework of *The Dark Tower* by combining three distinct genres—the Western, the Gothic tale and the apocalyptic fable.

King's fondness for mixing genres and playing them off against one another in his work reveals itself in *The Dead Zone* (1979), where he blends the supernatural with the conventions of the political novel, and in *Firestarter* (1980), where the dark fantastic joins with the espionage thriller.[2] Yet *The Dark Tower* stands out as the most complex generic mixture he has yet attempted. King has reworked the conventions and stereotypes of several literary idioms to express contemporary concerns.[3] Not only does *The Dark Tower* suggest King's versatility as a writer, but the story points to his ability to sustain and enrich a theme: King's modifications of the Western and Gothic genres consistently illustrate the controlling apocalyptic motif of the novel.

King does not borrow from a specific Western story, though general parallels to those which feature a gunslinger are obvious. Zane Grey and his imitators made the formula Western so pervasive that tracing King's specific sources becomes virtually impossible. To be sure, King does allude to Wister's *The Virginian* when Roland, his protagonist, says, "I hope he smiled when he said it" (55), referring to a remark made by his antagonist, the Man in Black. The allusion, of course, echoes the Virginian's famous line, "When you call me that, *smile*," directed at his rival, Trampas. This allusion to Wister notwithstanding, King's awareness of stock Western heroes and villains need not have come from printed sources at all, for as Sanford Marovitz points out, nearly anyone "remotely familiar with the horse-hoof-and-gunsmoke movies and romances of the twentieth century" can conjure up a Western badman.[4]

Despite the difficulty of identifying particular sources, a review of the generic features of the formula Western indicates how clearly King understands the formula. John Cawelti has isolated the primary qualities of the typical Western setting. Obviously, the Western takes place in the West, near the frontier. The second paragraph of *The Dark Tower* establishes an appropriately Western setting: "The desert was the apotheosis of all deserts, huge, standing to the sky for what might have been parsecs in all directions. White; blinding; waterless; without feature save for the faint, cloudy haze of the mountains which sketched themselves on the horizon..." (11). Virtually the entire action of the novel takes place in either an open desert or mountain region, with the exception of several other settings which are likewise characteristic of Westerns— a saloon in a ramshackle town, an abandoned stagecoach station and a forgotten railroad line. The desert offers the "openness...aridity and general inhospitability" which, Cawelti claims, are also mainstays of Western outdoor scenery. The extremes of climate which frequently figure in the Western are represented by the parched, blindingly bright desert and the cold, narrow mountain passage through which Roland must travel. Desert and mountain terrain, however, are more than literal Western landscapes. As the plot makes clear, King evokes a "symbolic" landscape where "challenge...can lead to a rebirth of heroic individual morality."[5]

Jenni Calder points out that a "mysterious stranger...is a standard figure in the [Western] myth," and the term "mysterious stranger" surely fits Roland the Gunslinger.[6] Roland's past, never fully revealed, is presented by means of episodic flashbacks, and the purpose of his journey across the desert and into the mountains remains shadowy throughout the novel. Roland acts outside of normal social codes,[7] giving Sylvia Pittson, an "evangelist," cause to rally the town of Tull against him. Like the gunslinger of many a Western tale and film, moreover, Roland is a lonely man. He sets out alone on his ambiguous quest and finally confronts the Man in Black alone. Roland chooses to leave behind Allie, a woman he has grown fond of in Tull, and Jake, a boy who accompanies him on part of the journey. Each, however, provides only a momentary respite from his chronic loneliness. Though Roland may be lonely, he also possesses the relentless endurance[8] shared by many other isolated figures, Shane and Grey's Lassiter among them, who wander the vast landscape of the Western. Ralph Willett argues that the "Westerner is a man with a gun. Whether an outlaw or a sheriff, he is violent." Roland carries a gun—he is, in fact the last Gunslinger, the last remnant of a knight-like order of Gunslingers, a curiosity even in the Western setting of *The Dark Tower*. Yet the Western hero in general, and Roland in particular, typically rises above the role of dispossessed shootist. The Gunslinger remains a craftsman, one who "does something well." Nor can he be reduced to a trigger-happy murderer, for his approach to killing may be described as "reluctant but aesthetic."[9] Many of the qualities of the conventional gunslinger can be found in Roland, particularly in Tull, where his craft constantly displays itself. Roland's air of quiet command becomes apparent as soon as he enters the saloon:

The man was halfway up behind him when the gunslinger saw him in the mirror. The man was almost completely bald, and his hand was wrapped around the haft of a gigantic hunting knife that was looped onto his belt like a holster. "Go sit down," the gunslinger said quietly. The man stopped. His upper lip lifted unconsciously, like a dog's, and there was a moment of silence. Then he went back to his table and the atmosphere shifted back again. (27-28)

Obviously, Roland knows his business—he has done something well, efficiently, by allowing the knife-wielder to contemplate what will probably happen unless he backs down quickly, instead of filling the man full of holes. Roland deftly uses the aura of power that the shootist, Shane notably, often possesses. When matters get more violent, Roland does not change essentially. After spending several days in Tull, he realizes that he will have to shoot because Sylvia Pittston has turned the entire town into a crazed vigilante mob intent on killing him:

He retreated, moving his body like a dancer to avoid the flying missiles. He reloaded as he went, with a rapidity that had also been trained into his fingers. They shuttled busily between gunbelts and cylinders. The mob came up over the boardwalk and he stepped into the general store and rammed the door closed. The large display window to the right shattered inward and three men crawled through. Their faces were zealously blank, their eyes filled with bland fire. He shot them all, and the two that followed them. (60)

Roland is violent, but not gratuitously so—he has a right to protect himself. He reacts "like a dancer" to the charging mob, shooting because he must, gracefully, acrobatically, aesthetically.

The Tull killings, moreover, represent King's use of another Western convention—sometimes the decadent town can enhance the moral status of the hero. In several ways Tull approximates the decadence of Lago in the film *High Plains Drifter* (1973). Most of the citizens in both towns are corrupt, cowardly and vicious. Tull contains little more than a collection of drifters, religious fanatics and "devil-grass" addicts who, unlike Roland, yearn to kill what they cannot understand. In this context, the shootist becomes, if not a hero, then at least a person who does the rest of civilization a service by disposing of its human debris. Roland does not glory in the carnage he leaves behind, nor does he waste tears on the zombie-like townspeople who have provoked their own deaths. Ultimately, Roland's actions in Tull suggest that he is morally superior to the "corruption of society." The Western hero in the typical adventure tale requires an enemy, who can range from the "personification of destructive evil," to a "personal rival,"[10] to a town such as Lago or Tull. In *The Dark Tower* Roland's primary enemy is the enigmatic Man in Black, not the town of Tull—the Man in Black had turned Tull against Roland, and then gone on his way. To right this wrong and several others which occurred earlier in his life, Roland pursues the shadowy antagonist. The Man in Black is simultaneously a personal enemy, the personification of evil and the holder of dark secrets which Roland will stop at nothing to learn. He remains a complex figure, a composite of the traits possessed by a multitude of "enemies" in Western stories.

The Dark Tower's plot contains several Western formula elements as well. First and foremost, the plot involves pursuit: Roland intends to learn the Man in Black's secrets by tracking him down. Most of the novel focuses on the tracking process and the overcoming of the obstacles the Man in Black has placed in Roland's way. Roland desires, above all, to keep moving, a desire which Cawelti finds abundant in Western plots and protagonists generally. Two other elements important to Western plots also figure in the story: the outlaw motif and the revenge motif. Roland's guns and freedom from "normal social codes" mark him as an "outlaw," the sort of person the citizens of Tull ironically consider to be an unruly lawbreaker from the "outside." His tenuous relationships with the "law," formal or informal, are crucial to the novel. Equally important, Roland seeks revenge, for he identifies the Man in Black as part of a conspiracy which dishonored Roland's father when Roland was a boy. Now Roland seeks to avenge his father's honor. Finally, *The Dark Tower's* plot makes use of a general motif found in countless Westerns. As did Wister and Grey, King sees the novel's Western setting and action as a testing ground for character and idea[11]—Roland's capabilities as a gunslinger, his concept of vengeance and his understanding of the alluring secrets his enemy possesses.

The Dark Tower, though, does not conform to many of the traditional patterns and values of generic Westerns. King modifies the Western formula in both minor and substantial ways, and these modifications not only establish his Western as distinctive, but point to its thematic direction as well. The Western hero, as Cawelti points out, is a "man with a horse." Neither Roland nor his adversary rides a horse, and herds of wild mustangs do not gallop along the horizon as they might do in a Grey story. Roland either walks or works the handle of a railroad handcar. Characteristically, someone plays the role of the savage, usually Indians or outlaws. In *The Dark Tower* Roland and Jake do confront the Slow Mutants, who attack their handcar, but neither Indians nor outlaws are present. The citizens of Tull come closest to the traditional notion of "savagery" when they charge Roland, yet townspeople do not fit comfortably into the pattern of savagery characteristic of the Western; that pattern is better represented by Apaches on the warpath, cattle rustlers or Missouri raiders. One expects clarity in a formula Western's conflict, but this is not the case with *The Dark Tower*. True, when Roland shoots down his attackers in Tull, clarity prevails—he has no choice but to defend himself from a demented mob. However, ambiguity permeates Roland's relationship with the Man in Black, for the two are in conflict but neither seeks the other's death. Moreover, the origins of their conflict, though partially related to Roland's desire to avenge his father's honor, cannot be traced simply to revenge. The Man in Black seems to be guiding Roland to a destination Roland wishes to arrive at. Additionally, in a formula Western "violence is characteristically the hero's means of resolving the conflict generated by his adversary."[12] The formula applies well enough to the Tull episodes and the fight with the Slow Mutants, but not to the confrontations with the Man in Black. At one point Roland spots his adversary and fires away at him, but the adversary merely laughs, warning Roland that bullets cannot resolve their differences. In fact, though Roland does not drop his guard, the two parlay in the last chapter, exchanging information rather than blows.

If "one of the major organizing principles of the Western is to so characterize the villains that the hero is both emotionally and intellectually justified in destroying them," then King departs substantially from the formula, and again his departure involves the Man in Black. Roland remains uncertain of his antagonist's identity and cannot prove him guilty of any crimes; the matter of "villainy" remains in question. Moreover, destroying the Man in Black would probably be intellectually foolish, even if his villainy were indisputable, because destruction would permanently deny certain truths to Roland. The formulaic act of destruction would likely prove emotionally frustrating as well—it would be an admission of futility and defeat. Assuming, as Cawelti does, that the "most basic definition of the hero role in the Western is as the figure who resolves the conflict between pioneers and savages," we can detect another basic modification of the pattern. As noted earlier, King blurs the issue of savages and savagery in *The Dark Tower*, and there are no "pioneers" in the remote areas through which Roland travels. At no point does he act as a mediator between conflicting groups, nor does he perceive himself as one. The essence of the formulaic definition of a Western hero, therefore, does not apply to Roland. If the Western formula absolves the hero from making complex choices because the formula "has been an artistic device for resolving problems rather than confronting their irreconcilable ambiguities," then King seems to modify the formula dramatically. As I shall argue later, Roland must confront a series of intricate choices, several of which have ambiguous, long-term consequences for him and for the human race itself. Few of the substantial problems he addresses offer any immediate hope of resolution. Cawelti's notion that in the formula Western the tragic magnitude of the hero shrinks because his "situation is linked to a particular period of history with its limited way of life" provides additional insights into King's pattern of departures from the formula. If anything, Roland's heroic potentialities are virtually the opposite of those allowed the conventional hero. His quest becomes so broad and complex that it transcends a particular setting or way of life, and his tragic-heroic stature expands proportionally. Confrontation and vengeance do motivate Roland, but discovering transcendent secrets motivates him more. In the broadest sense, a formula story provides its readers with "a clear and reassuring regularity" and follows a straightforward and fairly predictable pattern of expectations. The "basic structure" of the Western, like that of virtually all formula stories, is one of "resolution and reaffirmation."[13] King seems intent on avoiding regularity, resolution and reaffirmation: Roland's quest often forces him to confront the opposite of these formulaic norms. *The Dark Tower's* generic and thematic impulses, in fact, typically disrupt the reader's pattern of expectations, offering him questions, not solutions.

One of the primary reasons why *The Dark Tower* departs so radically from the reader's pattern of expectations may be that King incorporates into his Western several major conventions of Gothicism, an idiom which cultivates open-ended ambivalence instead of resolution. The Gothic qualities of the novel support the idea that King presents his West mythically and metaphorically rather than realistically. One finds in *The Dark Tower* some of the features of the dark fantastic which dominate King's other works. Gothic elements do, of course, appear in more than one Western. Jenni Calder notes that the West's dying towns have a "gothic quality."[14] King's Gothicism stands out emphatically in the many traces of the unexplained supernatural one finds.[15] The Slow Mutants, repulsive humanoid creatures who live in darkness, slime and stagnant water, feed like jungle carnivores, and never leave the shadowy realms beneath the earth, resemble the monsters common in Gothic tales. Early in the novel Roland hears an eerie voice beckoning to him; he digs into the wall of an abandoned stagecoach stop and discovers a skeleton, the apparent source of the voice. Roland takes the jawbone of the skeleton and later uses it as a supernatural divining rod. Midway through the story, the Gunslinger meets an oracle trapped in an enchanted circle of stones; in exchange for Roland's sexual favors the spirit foretells his future. Clearly, the oracle resembles the supernatural seer figure of Gothic tradition. Moreover, the Man in Black appears to be an occult character disguised by a hooded, monkish robe. His powers are considerable, but he cannot be called a priest or an agent of the divine, though he poses as both. In the last chapter of *The Dark Tower* he does a Tarot reading for the Gunslinger. The Man in Black claims to be the "furthest minion of the Dark Tower" (205-06), one lowly member of what Roland considers to be a powerful, ageless, occult hierarchy. All of these signs point to the probability that the Man in Black is not human.

Several of the story's organizing motifs have a Gothic ring to them as well. Roland journeys into the nightland, into the dark side of experience, rather than into the bright sunshine and the Promised Land of the conventional Western. His journey involves a typically Gothic predicament—he sets out into an immense unknown territory, and that territory is probably expanding, not stationary. The Gothic motif of the double permeates *The Dark Tower*. The Gunslinger and the Man in Black do appear different at first, yet they eventually prove quite similar. Each has information and powers that the other desires. Roland tries to shoot the Man in Black, but his antagonist warns Roland that Roland cannot do so without killing himself. Essentially the same motif appears in such Gothic classics as Poe's "William Wilson" and Wilde's *The Picture of Dorian Gray*. King's metaphysics of the dark fantastic reads like a contemporary rendering of concepts that have permeated Gothicism for more than two centuries: the primordial power and pervasiveness of the unknown, the irrationality and unpredictability of the human psyche and the moral reality of good and evil. Like the Western, the Gothic story "may evoke an image of the lonely, isolated self pressing onward despite all obstacles, while either indulging or struggling with an internal evil." Though Roland wanders across a landscape like that of the Western, the Gothic elements of *The Dark Tower* suggest that he has entered a Gothic universe which offers "shadowy semblances of an occult order but withholds final revelation and illumination."[16]

King uses the Western and the Gothic tale to establish a framework for Roland's quest, and the two genres constantly interact and reinforce one another. Gothic elements help to make *The Dark Tower* a "new," surrealistic Western. The frontier of the conventional Western moves closer to the psychological shadowland of the Gothic tradition; the closure and resolution so characteristic of formulaic Westerns opens out into the ambivalence of Gothicism; even the landscape typical of the two genres has begun to overlap: the Gunslinger travels *across* a Western desert, but *towards* a Gothic building, the Dark Tower. In short, King sets his hero on a quest from the known and relatively familiar territory of the West into the dark reaches of infinity. Ostensibly different, the two genres still share an important linking characteristic. If the Western is a *mythos* of Quest Romance, so also is the Gothic, the principal distinction being the enigmatic quality of the Gothic quest. Formula Westerns may be Romantic parables,[17] but Gothicism stands as a primary example of Dark Romanticism. The Gothic features of *The Dark Tower* do not contradict its Western qualities but extend them instead, so that the two genres define and explore the limits of one another.

Perhaps more importantly, the Western and the Gothic both contribute substantially overall to the apocalyptic allegory which unifies the seemingly disparate elements of *The Dark Tower*. One commonly associates apocalypse with total destruction or "cosmic wreckage," the end of the world and the post-catastrophic scene. However, as John Ketterer demonstrates, apocalypse invariably celebrates a "grand new world" because the apocalyptic paradigm is circular. Scripture, particularly the Book of Revelation, provides most of the familiar apocalyptic images and themes. Apocalyptic literature forms a dialectical tension of opposites: "existence itself is at stake—antinomies of life and death, light and darkness, knowledge and nescience, order and chaos." Apocalyptic motifs permeate *The Dark Tower*.[18] The setting provides clues that Roland's world differs greatly from the more complex, technological, "modern" world which preceded it. As he sets out across the desert, Roland follows an ancient highway (13). During his crossing, he must carefully avoid the ubiquitous devil-grass, an addictive narcotic which seems to be the product of nuclear radiation. In the underground railroad terminal he passes through, Roland finds military insignia lying next to skeletons, and a mummified body, causing him to remark, "Gas...they used to be able to make a gas that would do this" (183). In the same terminal, a "converter was turning the air over and over, as it had for thousands of years..." (182). The medieval "court" at which Roland grew up suggests that civilization has been overturned and is slowly trying to right itself again—the court's cook owns one of only six working appliances left from the earlier time (100). Generally, then, Roland inhabits a post-apocalyptic environment made up of technological leftovers, medieval customs and frontier conditions like those of the Old West. Northrop Frye's analysis of demonic apocalyptic imagery underscores the apocalyptic qualities of Roland's world. At several points on the journey Roland encounters ruins or the equivalent of "catacombs." The immense desert represents the "vast, menacing" powers of nature which now prevail. Monsters are present, as the Slow

Mutants, the probable offspring of nuclear war, make abundantly clear. Frye maintains that the dominant social relation of demonic apocalypse "is that of the mob," and the largest group of people Roland encounters is the crazed mob that chases him through Tull.[19]

King's characterization fits equally well into the apocalyptic paradigm. Most of Tull's inhabitants are convinced that the "Last Times" are near (50). In their midst lives the grotesquely fat, slug-like Sylvia Pittston, who came out of the desert and now lives where the "real" minister used to live (53). Pittston alludes to the "Interloper," to the coming of the Last Times, and turns Tull against Roland by claiming he is the Antichrist. Roland shoots Pittston, a minion of the character he cannot shoot, the Man in Black, who possesses many of the traits of the shape-shifting demonic trickster of apocalyptic lore. Jake thinks of the Man in Black as a priest because of his robe and hood (76), but Roland cannot clearly identify his antagonist. Early on he thinks that Marten, an opponent of his at court, may be the half-brother of the Man in Black; later Roland becomes convinced that the Man in Black is Walter, someone he had known at court. The Man in Black's powers further complicate the question of his identity. In the Tull saloon he performs a demonic parody of Christ's Resurrection by raising Nort, a decrepit devil-grass addict, from the dead, convincing the town of his "divine" capabilities. When he and Roland sit down to parlay, the Man in Black magically lights the campfire. Then he puts Roland in a trance and gives him a Genesis-like vision of the world's creation and a glimpse of the Dark Tower. Collectively, the Man in Black's actions identify him as a manipulative demonic agent, the apocalyptic False Prophet.

Roland's character and allegorical quest fit comfortably into the apocalyptic scenario of *The Dark Tower*. From the beginning of the story, Roland is identified as a unique, powerful individual, one who knows the ancient High Speech and can command the lower orders of demons. Still, he must pass several tests to prove his worthiness for a great task. The desert wastes he passes through are referred to as "purgatorial" (13)—he must survive them. The Man in Black makes Roland's task more difficult by placing several human obstacles in his way. Roland must abandon Allie, the woman he had begun to love in Tull; then he must conquer his lust for the monstrous Pittson; finally, Roland must abandon the boy John Chambers, whose initials suggest much, in order to continue his search for the Man in Black. Moreover, Roland needs to sharpen his psychic awareness so that he can take the measure of the Gothically transformed post-apocalyptic world. The narrator observes that Roland has a "lack of imagination" (150) and that "meditation was a new thing for him" (138). True, Roland possesses mystical qualities—he can commune with the oracle in the way station and the spirit in the enchanted circle. Yet in order to deal with the Man in Black and the mysteries of the Tower he must become more mystically sensitive. The Gothic qualities of his environment become part of the test by acting to deepen Roland's sensitivity. When he finally confronts the Man in Black, Roland faces one of his most difficult tasks, for the Man in Black is more like Roland than Roland would care to admit. To accentuate this similarity, references to the double permeate their conversation (192, 198). Before the quest can continue, Roland has to reckon with his own dark side and its ominous possibilities, especially the possibility that he has been avoiding this confrontation. The Man in Black is not precisely Roland's alter ego, but rather the embodiment of what Roland might become, the sum of his negative capabilities. Roland's "double" warns him that searching for the Tower means risking his own soul because the Beast controls the Tower and Roland will be required to slay him—failure means forfeiture of Roland's soul. After he has endured the dream vision of the Tower, Roland earns the right to continue the quest.

Even though Roland faces peril, a sense of urgency moves him as he repeatedly contemplates the fact that "the world has moved on." Roland's post-apocalyptic world waits, desolate and decadent, for rebirth and integration, waits for freedom from the apocalypse that was and the apocalypse that may be. Roland searches amidst chaos for order, working to find meaning and purpose in his environment, and recognizing that a metaphysical transformation must precede any other kind. Roland's quest, then, is to bring renewal to a wasteland, though he may die in the process. His quest, finally, suggests the circular quality of the apocalyptic paradigm—Roland's behavior signals a break with the enervated decadence of the land he inhabits. He embodies the qualities of those who are able to come to terms with metaphysical realities in the post-apocalyptic wasteland: courage, radical individualism, mystical awareness and the willingness to confront God and/or infinity. These qualities mark the beginning of a "grand new world."

The apocalyptic features of *The Dark Tower* would seem to alter fundamentally its nature as a Western, but such is not the case. Instead, apocalypticism acts as an epic magnification of several key elements of the Western formula. Cawelti argues that the frontier has great potential for exciting, epic conflicts, and Roland's clash with the minions of the Dark Tower surely qualifies as that sort of conflict. The principal difference between the conflicts of a formula Western and those of *The Dark Tower* appears to be one of scale—Roland strives to save the human race from an apocalyptic explosion which may wipe out the species altogether. Apocalypticism likewise expands the tragic magnitude of the hero's role in the novel. Cawelti's claim that the formula Western's hero has limited tragic possibilities because of the historical limitations of his situation does not apply to King's story because Roland's situation allows him the chance to act, as humankind's knight-errant, in a way that transcends historical limitations: should Roland fail to unravel the mysteries of the Tower, he will fail for all of his fellow men and possibly for all time. Implicit parallels between cowboys and knights are commonplace in Western literature; King makes the parallel more explicit. If, as Calder maintains, we "can think of the mythic West as a gigantic battlefield where every man has to prove himself as a warrior," the difference between *The Dark Tower* and the formula Western again becomes primarily one of scale. Like the Tower itself, Roland's battlefield is cosmic and timeless; thus his warrior-like deeds have the appropriate transcendent quality. Cowboy heroes such as the Virginian, Shane and Lassiter successfully resist a series of temptations, and Roland does the same. Roland's temptations, of course, tend to be more grandiose. Even the formulaic identity of the gunfighter remains recognizable in King's Western. In the "typical story," James Folsom points out, "the professional gunfighter sells his skill...to someone else for wages"; but another option exists: the gunfighter can "remain unattached to any party, true to some kind of a vision of moral justice" and a freedom of moral action. Roland's behavior fits the second option—he remains true to his quest, and his guns are not for hire. Finally, King's use of a frontier setting recalls a major element in the formula Western. Roland fits the mythic framework of the formula because he is a pathfinder and a trailblazer in the post-apocalyptic wilderness. Since the new frontier can be elusively mystical at times, Roland must display the sort of sensitivity toward the environment that Cooper's Leatherstocking did. Civilization having been reduced to a "simpler level," opportunities for heroic "quests and individual action" are abundant for Roland just as they are for typical gunslingers in conventional Westerns. If the frontier can be defined as a "simple, mystical, non-technological world,"[20] then Roland's post-apocalyptic environment represents the adaptation of the formulaic Western setting to another time and place. *The Dark Tower*, in short, evokes the West rather than obliterating it.

Notes

[1] *The Dark Tower: The Gunslinger* (West Kingston, Rhode Island: Donald Grant, 1982) 219. Future references will be included in the text.

[2] See my "Antidetection: Gothic and Detective Conventions in the Fiction of Stephen King," *Clues: A Journal of Detection* 5 (1984): 131-46.

[3]John G. Cawelti, *The Six-Gun Mystique* (Bowling Green: Popular Press, 1971) 36. My debts to Cawelti's theories about formula Westerns are substantial and will be acknowledged in detail throughout the essay. Cawelti's two studies have brilliantly demonstrated the usefulness of defining conventions and stereotypes in a genre.

[4]Marovitz, "Frontier Conflicts: Villains, Outlaws, and Indians in Selected 'Western' Fiction: 1799-1860," diss., Duke University, 1968, 241.

[5]Cawelti, *Six-Gun Mystique* 39-41; Cawelti, *Adventure, Mystery, and Romance: Formula Stories as Art and Popular Culture* (Chicago: U of Chicago Press, 1976) 241.

[6]Calder, *There Must Be a Lone Ranger* (London: Hamish Hamilton, 1974) 18.

[7]James K. Folsom, *The American Western Novel* (New Haven: College and University Press, 1966) 138.

[8]Calder 1, 16.

[9]Willett, "The American Western: Myth and Anti-Myth," *Journal of Popular Culture* 4 (1970): 457; Folsom 125; Cawelti, *Six-Gun Mystique* 60.

[10]Calder 17; Folsom 125; Calder 200.

[11]Cawelti, *Six-Gun Mystique* 31; Cawelti 64; Russel Nye, *The Unembarrassed Muse: The Popular Arts in America* (New York: Dial Press, 1970) 300; Cawelti, *Formula Stories* 235.

[12]Cawelti, *Six-Gun Mystique* 57; Cawelti 52; Nye 301; Cawelti 24.

[13]Cawelti, *Six-Gun Mystique* 14; Cawelti 55; Cawelti 37; Cawelti 56; Cawelti 51; Cawelti 71; Cawelti 73.

[14]Calder 71.

[15]King admits in his Afterword how much Robert Browning's poem "Childe Roland to the Dark Tower Came" influenced his own work (221). The Gothic qualities of Browning's poem, I believe, are the essence of King's borrowing, particularly the solitary adventurer named Roland, the shadowy figures he meets on his journey to the tower and the enigmatic tower itself.

[16]G.R. Thompson, ed., *The Gothic Imagination: Essays in Dark Romanticism* (Pullman: Washington State UP, 1974) 1, 6.

[17]Cawelti, *Six-Gun Mystique* 68-70; Folsom 125-28.

[18]R.W.B. Lewis, *Trials of the Word: Essays in American Literature and the Humanistic Tradition* (New Haven: Yale UP, 1965) 184; Ketterer, *New Worlds For Old: The Apocalyptic Imagination, Science Fiction, and American Literature* (New York: Doubleday, 1974) 10; John R. May, *Toward a New Earth: Apocalypse in the American Novel* (South Bend, Notre Dame Press, 1971) 19; for a discussion of apocalypse in King's other novels, see my "Apocalypticism in the Fiction of Stephen King," *Extrapolation: A Journal of Science Fiction and Fantasy* 25 (1984): 214-27.

[19]Frye, *Anatomy of Criticism: Four Essays* (Princeton: Princeton UP, 1957) 147-50.

[20]Cawelti, *Six-Gun Mystique* 59; Calder 134; Folsom 125; Gary K. Wolfe, *The Known and the Unknown: The Iconography of Science Fiction* (Kent: Kent State UP, 1979) 146.

Taking Stephen King Seriously: Reflections on a Decade of Best-Sellers

Samuel Schuman

I.

I am not sure what it was that first suggested to me the notion that Stephen King was an author to be taken seriously. Three things happened in the late 1970's that somehow, separately or together, brought me to that rather unconventional conclusion.

First, I (and everyone else) began to notice that not only were King's works perpetual best-sellers, he was also beginning to generate multiple, overlapping works at the top of the popularity charts. Indeed, in 1980, King became the first American author to have *three* works simultaneously on the best-seller lists—*Fire Starter, The Dead Zone*, and *The Shining*. When I first began to contemplate writing this paper, King appeared in the most recent *New York Times* lists (Sunday, Feb. 3, 1985) for hardcover books (#3, *The Talisman*, written with Peter Staub) and paperbacks (#9, *Pet Sematary*). Today (Spring, 1987), *Misery* tops the best-seller charts, while the movie *Stand By Me*, was the sleeper hit of the fall cinema season, and the author graces the cover of *Time* magazine. ANYTHING so popular for so long merits attention, whether it is Stephen King, the Beatles, the Ford Mustang, or Wm. Shakespeare.

Second, it was at about this same time that I met the author and had a (minor) opportunity to work with him. I was a new administrator at the University of Maine at Orono. King had graduated from that school, and, after his initial successes and, therefore, long after there was any financial incentive to do so, he offered to return to his alma mater for a year of teaching literature and writing. Since we were both affiliated with the English Department, we served on some committees together, and brushed up against each other in the studiedly casual way departmental colleagues do in larger American universities. Since we shared, as well, one very good friend—Dr. Ulrich Wicks, then Chair of the English Department—I had an opportunity to meet King on a number of social occasions. Although we were never particularly close, proximity to fame (of almost any sort) breeds a kind of respect and interest.

Thirdly, and most importantly, I began to take Stephen King seriously in the late 1970's because that was when, in a totally unstructured and non-academic way, I began to read his books.

II.

Given King's unprecedented record of success—in film and television, as well as in print—it seems evident that anyone seriously interested in the state of contemporary American taste must pay substantial attention to his work. However, although King has written a lengthy work of criticism, holds a baccalaureate degree in English, and has taught literature, he is not much given to respectful kowtowing to the lit-crit establishment, and academic critics are certainly not enamored of his works. The general response to King's ouvre amongst academics has been to ignore it or to consider it beneath contempt. Very occasionally, a literate reviewer will offer a back-handed compliment. [e.g., "King is too powerful a writer to go on indefinitely slinging his ink in cinematic verbal effects to no purpose. He has shown an acute understanding of human fears; if he can move toward an equally profound apprehension of our hopes, he may yet write a book that transcends its genre in the manner of all true art." Mary H. Rosenbaum, *Christian Century* 101, (March 21-8, 1984) p. 316.]

I want to suggest that, in fact, Steve King is a master of plot and setting; a skillful and self-conscious manipulator of the English language; a rather stern moralist; and a first-class creator of literary characters. King is not, and probably will not become, the Shakespeare of our day [although, as we all know, Shakespeare was not the "Shakespeare" of his day, either, if by that denomination we mean a recognized master of literary art—Shakespeare and his fellows in the Elizabethan theater were seen by educated and literary folk as popular hacks]. His greatest flaw seems to be the same that Shakespeare—and Dickens and Thomas Wolfe—suffered from: he has a tendency to churn out enormous volumes of prose with great speed and without much of an inclination to go back over what he has written and make sure he has got everything just right. As a consequence, he is often "uneven." Portions of his works give the impression of immaculate craftsmanship, but they will be interspersed with other portions which are awkward, sloppy, hasty, and obviously not of very much interest to their author.

King's second major problem is a fairly regular and deliberate absence of taste. King seems to be the only important current writer other than Norman Mailer who can be very obscene without coming anywhere near the pornographic. He himself says that, when he can not achieve a higher effect, he will aim at revulsion:

> ...I will try to terrorize the reader. But if I find I cannot terrify him/her, I will try to horrify; and if I find I cannot horrify, I'll go for the gross-out. I'm not proud. (*Danse Macabre*, p. 25)

This is an accurate description, and sometimes King seems too good at achieving this end. [One could make a case that in certain scenes Shakespeare seems to be "going for the gross-out," too. The cry of "Out, vild jelly" by Cornwall as he plucks out Gloucester's one remaining eye falls into this class (*King Lear* III. vii. 83). So does the scene in *Cymbeline* in which Imogen mistakes the body of Cloten for that of Posthumus—because it is without a head (*Cymbeline*, IV. ii. 295 ff, the lines and stage directions make it mandatory for Imogen to fondle and, finally, collapse upon, the gruesome corpse). So too does the scene in *Titus Andronicus* in which the ravished Lavinia, who has had her hands cut off and her tongue cut out, reveals the names of her rapists with this ingenious device: "She takes the staff in her mouth, and guides it with her stumps, and writes" (IV. i. 77 sd). Still, such scenes are the exceptions in Shakespeare's plays, and seem unfortunately common in King's novels. In this regard, he is perhaps akin less to the Bard of Avon than to Webster or Tourneur.]

III.

In spite of these weaknesses, I believe Stephen King is a gifted and even important writer. To me, his particular strengths are:

—a surprisingly effective prose style, especially in the area of descriptive composition and dialogue;

—an ability to create characters at once unique and universal, and who therefore interest and engage us;

—a strong and clear ethical stance, which often generates a reassuring thematic message;

—most importantly, an ability to imagine and represent plots which is absolutely brilliant.

Perhaps the best manner to illustrate these gifts is through a somewhat detailed look at one particular bestseller. Because I find it his most effective novel, overall, I have selected *Pet Sematary* (1983).

IV.

I think there are few if any descriptive passages in the English language that are any finer than this [the first paragraph of Shirley Jackson's *The Haunting of Hill House*]; it is the sort of quiet epiphany every writer hopes for: words that somehow transcend words, words which add up to a total greater than the sum of the parts.

Analysis of such a paragraph is a mean and shoddy trick, and should almost always be left to college and university professors, those lepidopterists of literature who, when they see a lovely butterfly, feel that they should immediately run into the field with a net, catch it, kill it with a drop of chloroform, and mount it.... Having said that, let us analyze this paragraph a bit. (*Danse Macabre*, p. 268)

It should be clear from this citation that Stephen King pays close attention to the niceties of English prose style. In particular, I believe that he works very hard, and usually quite successfully, at building exactly the sort of descriptive passage he praises in Shirley Jackson's work—the description which not only tells the reader *exactly* what some locale looks like, but goes beyond to convey its mood and its meaning. Here, for example, is the description of the pet cemetery which becomes a most important spot in the book named after it. *Pet Sematary*'s hero, Louis Creed, a physician and a newcomer to Maine, is taken, with his family in tow, to this spot by a native Mainer, on a pleasant weekend day outing:

They topped the second hill, and then the path sloped through a head-high swatch of bushes and tangled underbrush. It narrowed and then, just ahead, Louis saw Ellie and Jud go under an arch made of old weatherstained boards. Written on these in faded black paint, only just legible, were the words PET SEMATARY.
He and Rachel exchanged an amused glance and stepped under the arch, instinctively reaching out and grasping each other's hands as they did so, as if they had come here to be married.
For the second time that morning Louis was surprised into wonder.
There was no carpet of needles here. Here was an almost perfect circle of mown grass, perhaps as large as forty feet in diameter. It was bounded by thickly interlaced underbrush on three sides and an old blowdown on the fourth, a jackstraw jumble of fallen trees that looked both sinister and dangerous. A man trying to pick his way through that or to climb over it would do well to put on a steel jock, Louis thought. The clearing was crowded with markers, obviously made by children from whatever materials they could beg or borrow—the slats of crates, scrapwood, pieces of beaten tin. And yet, seen against the perimeter of low bushes and straggly trees that fought for living space and sunlight here, the very fact of their clumsy manufacture, and the fact that humans were responsible for what was here, seemed to emphasize what symmetry they had. The forested backdrop lent the place a crazy sort of profundity, a charm that was not Christian but pagan. (*Pet Sematary*, p. 42)

Without bludgeoning these lines to death, it seems to me that this is a masterful description. The clearing in the woods is described precisely: we know its dimensions, its boundaries, its entrance, the character of the forest floor. King also conveys the *age* of this space—the boards are "old" and "weatherstained," the printing upon them is "faded." The underbrush is "head-high" and the trees "straggly." The blowdown is an "old blowdown." The passage is, obviously, emotionally loaded—

the underbrush is "tangled" then "thickly interlaced." The jumble of trees is sinister and dangerous—it is dangerous in a way which makes the hero think about injury to his genitals. Vegetation fights for living space. But, along with this dense, dark, botanical aura, is a heavy emphasis upon the artifice of the cemetery—the grass is mown, the circle is "almost perfect." Items are "manufactured," "symmetrical." Obviously, King is trying to create a sense of a space which is at once childlike, a realistic man-made spot in the midst of the wild woods, and reverberating with a distinctly un-childish but also irrational and un-adult ominous sacramental presence. This is perhaps most effectively conveyed by the way in which the *Creeds* (their cat is named "Church!") *instinctively* hold hands, as if prepared for a rite, when they enter the cleared circle.

[As the novel develops, it turns out that the "PET SEMATARY" itself is not the "bad place"—the really haunted spot in the woods. Rather, that venue is on the other side of the sinister and dangerous blowdown. The cemetery serves as a gateway to the novel's site of genuine horror.]

This sense of a cleared spot in the midst of very rough forest which is not actively evil, but is certainly in no sense friendly or good, and which is invested with a distinctly non-Christian supernatural aura has literary precedents in similar locations in, for example, Hawthorne and "Gawain and the Green Knight."

Briefly, I also want to suggest that King's style is particularly sharp in the creation of dialogue. He has an excellent ear for the nuances of contemporary casual American speech, and he reproduces those rhythms and diction tellingly:

"Louis!" Rachel called. "She's cut herself!"
Eileen had fallen from the tire swing and hit a rock with her knee. The cut was shallow....
"All right, Ellie," he said. "That's enough. Those people over there will think someone's being murdered."
"*But it hurrrrts!*"
Louis struggled with his temper and went silently back to the wagon. The...first aid kit was still in the glove compartment. He got it and came back. When Ellie saw it, she began to scream louder than ever.
"*No! Not the stingy stuff! I don't want the stingy stuff, Daddy! No—*"
"Eileen, it's just Mercurochrome, and it doesn't sting—"
"*No-no-no-no-no—*"
"You want to stop that or your ass will sting," Louis said.
"She's tired, Lou," Rachel said quietly.
"Yeah, I know the feeling. Hold her leg out."
(*Pet Sematary*, pp. 18-19)

The progression from "Ellie" to "Eileen" to "you want to stop that..." catches exactly Louis' mounting irritation, and sounds precisely like most any other harassed father in a similar situation.

Stephen King, is, in sum, a compositional craftsman. In dialogue and description, particularly, he is precise, controlled, evocative. In *Danse Macabre*, he notes:

> ...many writers of fiction seem totally unable to explain simple operations or actions clearly enough for the reader to be able to see them in his or her mind's eye. Some of this is a failure on the writer's part to visualize well and completely; his or her own mind's eye seems bleared half-shut. More of it is a simple failure of that most basic writer's tool, the working vocabulary. If your're writing a haunted-house story and you don't know the difference between a gable and a gambrel, a cupola and a turret, paneling and wain-scotting, you, sir or madame, are in trouble. (p. 361)

V.

For "fright fiction" to work most effectively, it must focus upon a rather particular sort of character. The horror writer's protagonists must be sufficiently virtuous to win our sympathy, but sufficiently imperfect to seem recognizably human. They must be on the one hand interesting and unique, and on the other, "normal" and typical—otherwise, the evils which beset them will not be fully frightening to a readership which is, by and large, normal and typical. King's characters adhere exactly to these specifications. They are overwhelmingly middle-class, protestant, white, Americans. They are interested in earning a comfortable living. They are dutiful fathers, mothers, and children. They will err occasionally, but their sins are not gigantic (although they can plunge them into enormous nightmares) and seem almost comfortably domestic. Louis Creed, for example, has a rather sharp temper; he is permanently estranged from his father-in-law; etc. On the other hand, he is willing to take what seem heroic risks to preserve the integrity of his family. He is interesting and mildly unusual: Creed is a physician, but he has given up private practice to become a University doctor in Maine.

The work's second major character is Judson Crandall. Crandall comes close to appearing a stereotypical "Bert and I" New Englander: he is kindly, wry, tough, a man of few words. He is sincere, helpful, knowledgeable. He is saved, though, from saintliness by several frailties about which much of the plot of *Pet Sematary* revolves: He is, for example, so proud of knowing the secret of the pet cemetery that he can't resist showing off by revealing it to Louis Creed. At a crucial point at the end of the novel, Crandall falls asleep when he should have been keeping watchful guard. A glint of egotism, and a touch of dotage save Jud Crandall from becoming a *Yankee*-magazine Mainer, and leave him an individual for whom we can feel great fondness, pity, and a touch of kinship.

VI

Stephen King's novels (again, like Shakespeare's plays) do not ask us to stretch our moral imaginations. On the contrary, most of his books solidly and reassuringly reinforce conventional, middle-of-the-road ethical positions. Thus, on the one hand, King's works allow us to indulge ourselves in some wild fictive escapades (and to derive voyeuristic thrills at some fairly gruesome incidents!). But these events are usually packaged within a thematic structure which reinforces main-line Western moral traditions.

The Stand, It, Fire Starter, Cujo, The Shining, Misery, The Talisman and *Christine* all fall solidly within the traditional structure of a battle between good and evil. Sometimes the evil is human, (e.g., *Misery, Fire Starter*) more commonly it is supernatural (*The Shining; It*), mechanical (*Christine*) or animal (*Cujo*).

Pet Sematary is, at its core, a version of the Frankenstein myth, the moral of which is that it is always immoral and very dangerous to tinker with the natural order of birth and death. The key to the story is an Micmac indian burying ground. Dead bodies buried in this bewitched spot return to the world of the living—but not exactly as they left. Depending upon how long they have been dead, they seem to take on an increasingly baleful and malevolent personality quite distinct from their original natures. Louis Creed is introduced to the Micmac Burial Ground by Jud Crandall after Creed's family's pet cat is hit by a car. Creed and Crandall make a midnight trip into the woods, bury the cat, and (like the old song) the next day, the cat comes back. It is sullen, it snaps, it smells bad, but it's back. Then Creed's young son is hit and killed by a speeding truck, and Creed exhumes him and carries his body to the magical burial place. The boy, like the cat, returns, but he was dead too long, and his child-body seems possessed by a maniacal and diabolic spirit. *Pet Sematary* is a long novel, and this summation does not do it justice. It should be clear, though, that the thematic center of the novel derives from the clear moral judgment that it is sinful for humans to tamper with mortality. Creed falls, through love, into a sin the mirror opposite of murder: he does not make the living into the dead; he tries to make the dead to live again, and in so doing brings down upon himself and his family a progressive nightmare from which there is no escape. Within a plot of considerable imaginative ambition, King embeds a thematic core which would be gratifying to the most ardent fundamentalist.

(It is worthy of note that the book begins with a citation from John's Gospel, in which Jesus announces his intention to raise Lazarus from the dead.)

VII.

Stephen King's final novelistic strength is perhaps his most obvious, and most important: he is a master of plot, to Aristotle the most essential literary element. Although it would be great sport to illustrate this point with extensive summaries of King's plots, that entertaining step is really unnecessary. The one fact upon which all his readers agree is that Steve King's novels are page-turners. Their plots are engrossing and engrossingly unfolded. Beyond this general appreciation, two points are worth making briefly:

First, it is noteworthy that King's plots tend to be original with each novel: he does not rewrite the same best-seller over and over again. While most (but not all) of his works involve some element of the supernatural, that element varies wildly: an innocent and cute little girl who can set things on fire by the power of her mind; a car with a murderous personality of its own; wintering-over in a haunted summer resort in the Colorado mountains; a mad dog; vampires; a word-processor which can delete and create real things as well as words. So far, at least, King's imagination has been fertile, and he has admirably resisted the temptation to go back to the same lucrative story time after time.

Second, I want to conclude by suggesting that King is a master (really as a consequence of all the elements discussed above) of the most essential feature of the horror writers craft: he embeds the weirdness and the horror of his plots within a framework of convincingly mundane realism. The bizarre is interwoven persuasively with the familiar. King's craftsmanlike compositional style, his solid grasp of character, and his mastery of plotting combine to draw us into a world which always seems comfortingly like our own. He makes the incredible credible: if there were a secret burial ground outside Orono, Maine, in which the dead could be brought back to half-life, *this* is exactly what it would be like.

This is an imaginary toad in a real garden. This is the essence of the fiction writer's craft, and it is more than enough reason to take Steven King very seriously.

A Dream of New Life:
Stephen King's *Pet Sematary*
as a Variant of *Frankenstein*

Mary Ferguson Pharr

Among the great Gothic writers, Mary Shelley has a niche at once secure and unique. Only an occasional novelist, this reticent wife of the most radical of Romantics was somehow the sole creator of the seminal Gothic myth of modern technology. She was only eighteen when she dreamt of the myth she would incarnate as *Frankenstein*. Yet her adolescent inspiration—her revelation that uncontrolled science made man more demonic than deific—was stunning in its newness, absolutely original in its time. There is no real way for modern readers to feel that originality, for Mary's style was never eloquent. Her book was from the beginning an elemental force rather than a rhetorical triumph. Today her revelation, for all the flaws in its expression, remains a force but one which instead of stunning its audience, strikes them as simply fundamental.

Today there is Stephen King, as prolific a writer as even a paperback publisher could want, and a man still carving his niche through best sellers into literature. Almost entirely derivative, King's popular culture genius lies in his ability to redesign standard Gothic lore, to interpret rather than to originate. Mary Shelley wrote just six novels in her 53 years; most of these works soon became obscure, but all that she needed was the first one. Stephen King, now entering his 40's, has well over a dozen novels still in print. Indeed, his production is such that in order to avoid glutting the market with his name, he has over the last several years published five books under the pseudonym Richard Bachman. How much of King/Bachman's work will survive him is uncertain, though some of it surely will. Nothing he has written thus far, however, will make the mark of *Frankenstein*. King is no Shelley, nor has her work his stylistic strength, his easy readability. Yet they both touch that seminal myth, she creating it in *Frankenstein* and he reworking it in *Pet Sematary*.

The nexus between the two novels—between their centuries, in effect—occurs in the dream of new life each presents, a dream both seductive and malefic, the stuff finally of nightmares made flesh.

The Shelleys lived much of their lives in legend, Mary even more than Percy. The circumstances of her youth sound more like fiction than fact: a famous mother dying in childbirth, a famous father gradually retreating into selfish isolation, a bright and pretty little girl misunderstood by her foolish stepmother—such was the Cinderella childhood of Mary Wollstonecraft Godwin. Cinderella grew into a girl whose adolescence was marked by an odd blend of romantic melodrama and genuine tragedy: the affair with the young, aristocratic, regrettably married poet; the father's fury at their flight (Mary pregnant and Percy ever optimistic that his wife would understand); their gypsy life abroad (punctuated by grief over the death of their first baby); the suicides of Mary's pathetic half-sister and Percy's never-understanding first wife (punctuated by Percy's refusal to take any blame for the deaths and Mary's maturing into an awareness of more than just blame, of the need for responsibility); their subsequent marriage and eventual exile in Italy (with them there were the fame of the just published *Frankenstein*, the infamy of Percy's poetic and personal reputation, and always, the shadow of death, taking their next two children as it had taken their first, as it would soon take Percy Bysshe Shelley). This was Mary Shelley's youth. It can be no wonder she had nightmares.

One of them led directly to *Frankenstein*. During the course of a rainy summer in 1816, Lord Byron suggested to his Genevan circle that they hold an informal ghost story contest. Unable to think of anything to match the imagination of the others, Mary felt the fool until one night she dreamt of a student kneeling over a hideous being, a travesty of man created by the student through science. Years later, in an introduction to the 1831 edition of *Frankenstein* and with a voice muted by time and grief, Mary said of her vision: "Frightful must it be; for supremely frightful would be the effect of any human endeavour to mock the stupendous mechanism of the Creator of the world."[1] The next day she began a story which became the central episode of her novel. At the time she may not have wholly believed in the element of fearful mockery she was to focus on fifteen years later. After all, in 1816 Percy was still alive and still her mentor, and Percy believed in Prometheus Unbound, in the human possibilities of transcending human limitations. But even as a teenager, Mary knew how death binds man in spite of all his efforts, and she would come to know much more about the ties of death in the year of *Frankenstein*. At the last, Victor Frankenstein is her Prometheus—not Percy's—a Modern Prometheus bound by science to nightmare, by her dream to a frightful myth that has yet to be discarded.

Just as the *Frankenstein* manuscript had its inception in that dream which helped to shape the rest of Mary Shelley's life, so is the Frankenstein Creature first formed by the dreams of its creator. Victor Frankenstein's early life is almost a paradigm of happiness, so much so that it would seem he should have little use for idle dreaming. Indeed, his childhood is as secure as his author's was not: Victor has both parents, two younger brothers, a flawless best friend, and above all, his orphaned cousin Elizabeth who is his more than sister, who is a kind of gift to him from those loving, all-providing parents. The domestic circle is perfect, inclusive, untouched. It is as if Mary simply inverted the insecurity of her own experience and offered the result as the ideal familial order. Nonetheless, she has Victor turn away from the suffocating enclosure of this perfect circle to search for the philosopher's stone and the elixir of life—all for the purest of motives: "wealth was an inferior object; but what glory would attend the discovery, if I could banish disease from the human frame, and render man invulnerable to any but a violent death!" (p. 34). By his dreams of glory, Victor will separate himself first from his family and then from the humanity which they represent.

The separation starts with death. When Victor is 17, his mother dies of scarlet fever and he leaves the protection of his Genevan home for the University of Ingolstadt. In the course of a few years he outstrips not only his peers (he really has no peers) but also his professors. So intrigued is he with his studies that he pays no visits to Geneva, to his family during all this time. A prodigy of what the age called natural philosophy, Victor discovers the secret of life and resolves to create a human being. That resolution is crucial to the Frankenstein myth, for it is a decision based on instinct, on enthusiasm rather than on reason. Rationally, Victor knows he should begin with something small, but his imagination is "too much exalted" (p. 48), too large for either caution or common sense. The boy scientist, the student genius, is again a dreamer.

He rationalizes these new dreams of glory by theorizing that the secret of life is just a prelude to the far greater secret of resurrection:

Life and death appeared to me ideal bounds, which I should first break through, and pour a torrent of light into our dark world. A new species would bless me as its creator and source; many happy and excellent natures would owe their being to me. No father could claim the gratitude of his child so completely as I should deserve their's [sic]. Pursuing these reflections, I thought, that if I could bestow animation upon lifeless matter, I might in process of time (although I now found it impossible) renew life where death had apparently devoted the body to corruption. (p. 49)

Such is the Frankenstein philosophy, not natural at all, but a philosophy of science usurping nature. The secret of life is a great secret but not the ultimate one. As a matter of everyday fact, a man and a woman can together give life. While it is true that Victor learns to bestow such life without a partner, he cannot restore it to the dead, not even to his own mother. So he looks to the complexity of scientific animation to lead to the divinity of reanimation. Not content just to be a single parent, this Prometheus yearns to be a god, "creator and source."

Obsessed with his burgeoning ego, Victor creates the Creature in an intense, extended trance. "I seemed," he recalls much later, "to have lost all soul or sensation but for this one pursuit" (p. 50). The trance frees him from conscience just as it has already freed him from familial duty: he tortures animals, dabbles among graves and in charnel houses, and disturbs "with profane fingers, the tremendous secrets of the human frame" (p. 50). Blinded by his dazzling vision of self-deification, he cannot see the deformity, the potential horror of the gigantic being he intends to animate. In this sense, Victor is a poor scientist, aware only of the immediate interest of his work and with no thought for its consequences. In dreams, of course, no one considers consequences.

In life, however, consequences come. As the Creature opens its eyes, Victor sees it as it is for the first time: "the beauty of the dream vanished, and breathless horror and disgust filled my heart" (p. 53). Terrified, he flees and falls into an exhausted sleep, this time to dream of death and decay:

I thought I saw Elizabeth, in the bloom of health, walking in the streets of Ingolstadt. Delighted and surprised, I embraced her; but as I imprinted the first kiss on her lips, they became livid with the hue of death; her features appeared to change, and I thought that I held the corpse of my dead mother in my arms; a shroud enveloped her form, and I saw the grave-worms crawling in the folds of the flannel. (p. 53)

The dream is both Freudian and prophetic: mother and lover become one, but one only in death, seen in its grossest manifestations. Mme. Frankenstein lived well and was buried with honor; even so, her son never understands the dishonor, the absolute obscenity of his own graveyard violations. Elizabeth loves her cousin purely and lives to become a Frankenstein. Yet when she finally takes that name by marriage, she embraces only evil. Elizabeth dies on her wedding night, dies in the arms not of her husband but of the Creature, his son, her killer. In effect, Victor's dream comes true, as his wife joins his mother in a circle of death. Mme. Frankenstein first leaves Victor who then abandons the Creature who in turn kills Elizabeth who thus leaves Victor—who created the Creature because Mme. Frankenstein left the family. In the dream

Victor sees Elizabeth as his mother, and he sees himself bring death to both mother and bride by the work he has begun for the express purpose of saving them. So the dream is as much a prophecy of doom as it is a fantasy of guilt.

For the Creature is somehow always unfinished, in its own words, "an abortion" (p. 219), a species not of nature and the result of an incomplete conception. Born out of corruption—both physical and moral—it can only bring death and decay to the Frankenstein family, its family and Victor's. One by one, the members drop, never knowing who to blame. Victor and the Creature know, of course: they blame each other, the son cursing its father for his irresponsible refusal to care for his creation, and the father damning his son for its bloody acts of revenge against the rest of the Frankensteins. In truth, they are both right. The Creature is not just a poor monster much abused by its mad maker; it is a reflection of an ethically empty imagination, and so it is morally empty itself.

The dream made flesh, then, is inevitably a nightmare, taking the dreamer not to divinity but to infamy, even insanity. And the darkest part of this nightmare is that Victor never really gives up on his original vision. As he lies dying, he tells an acquaintance his life's story. Then he adds,

Farewell, Walton! Seek happiness in tranquillity, and avoid ambition, even if it be only the apparently innocent one of distinguishing yourself in science and discoveries. Yet why do I say this? I have myself been blasted in these hopes, yet another may succeed. (p. 215)

So Victor dies, trying to lure another into his fantasy. He dies unfulfilled, unable even to destroy that which he created. That creation, however, promises of its own accord to follow its father into death where "My spirit will sleep in peace; or if it thinks, it will not surely think thus" (p. 221). Finally "lost in darkness and distance" (p. 221), the Creature and its Creator alike dream unto extinction. There is no resurrection.

But there is in *Pet Sematary*. In a sense, Stephen King is always concerned with resurrection, with reviving the old lore of Dark Romanticism and incorporating it into the mass culture of late 20th-century America. The genesis of *Pet Sematary*, according to King's biographer Douglas Winter, lies in the author's interest in funeral customs, an interest seemingly sparked in 1979 by the death of the family cat. The cat in question was run over on a Maine highway so busy as to be a sort of "pet cemetery" for all kinds of unlucky animals. On finding and burying his pet, King began to think about burial itself:

He began to collect and study books on funerals and burial customs.... King pondered what would happen if someone buried a dead cat on a remote plot of land that had become a pet cemetery, and the cat magically came back to life. And then, if that someone's son were suddenly killed in a car accident.... The result, consciously twisting W.W. Jacobs' classic short story "The Monkey's Paw" (1902) is *Pet Sematary*.[2]

In *Danse Macabre* King himself speaks of the terror raised by Jacobs' story, which he regards as among the finest of its kind:

It's what the mind sees that makes these stories such quintessential tales of terror. It is the unpleasant speculation called to mind when the knocking on the door begins in ["The Monkey's Paw"] and the grief-stricken old woman rushes to answer it. Nothing is there but the wind when she finally throws the door open...but what, the mind wonders, *might* have been there if her husband had been a little slower on the draw with that mind wish?[3]

Terror is, as King notes, in the mind; but the irony of Jacobs' story is that what might have been outside that door is not truly in doubt in any reader's mind. What must have been there was a nightmare, walking death, the ground-up son become a variation on the Frankenstein Creature. Elsewhere in *Danse Macabre* King refers to Mary Shelley's work as "caught in a kind of cultural echo chamber."[4] Surely, one of those echoes is *Pet Sematary*, the book in which the author explicitly opens the door Jacobs left closed and lets that which was outside shamble in.

King has written more than one introduction for editions of *Frankenstein* and seems to feel an uneasy respect for a work both less vivid and more important than anything he has yet produced.[5] He has expressed that respect in diverse—and sometimes curious—ways (e.g., the "Frankenstein Monster" appears with almost every other famous monster in his novel *IT*). What King has done in *Pet Sematary* is not to copy Mary Shelley, but rather to amplify the cultural echo she set in motion so that its resonance is clearer to the somewhat jaded, not always intellectual reader of Gothic fantasy today. His is the best—perhaps because the least self-conscious—variant on her theme of the last 50 years.

Like Mary Shelley, King is domestic by nature. Like her as well, he was raised by only one parent (his father abandoned the family when Stephen was two years old). Unlike William Godwin, however, Nellie King worked hard for her children, who still must have felt a certain insecurity as they watched their mother struggle to make ends meet. The adult King married, had a family of his own, and found himself in danger of becoming a cliché: that is, an unpublished novelist turned teacher, a would-be writer eking out an existence with his wife and children packed into a trailer. Then came *Carrie*, and like the Shelleys, the Kings found fame young.

Despite it, despite the *People* magazine articles and the American Express commercial, King has remained a particularly devoted family man, who when asked the worst thing that he could ever imagine, replied it would be to find one of his children dead.[6] All children have a central, saving grace in King's novels: they are the heroes of *'Salem's Lot, The Shining, Firestarter,* and *The Talisman.* But even children can be changed, or so at least *Pet Sematary* suggests. Perhaps because of that suggestion, King left this manuscript unfinished for years, saying of it later, "I had written something that was so horrible that I didn't want to deal with it on a redraft...."[7] A contract dispute with Doubleday changed his mind, and he let loose on the public that worst thing he could ever imagine. As did Mary Shelley, he took his readers into his nightmares.

Or rather, since his is a recurring dream, he *takes* his readers—by a route that leads through the pages of *Pet Sematary.* Its central figure, Dr. Louis Creed, is a physician newly arrived in Maine. He has left his urban background in Chicago to start a new life as director of medical services at the University of Maine. The epitome of normalcy, he certainly seems at first no Victor Frankenstein. For one thing, he is already married, the father of two small children. For another, he is clearly in love with his wife and content with his profession. Even so, there are flaws. Louis sometimes daydreams of escape, of dumping his entire family when they become too loud, too irritating, just too hard to put up with. Then he fantasizes about abandoning his burdens and driving south, "all the way to Orlando, Florida, where he would get a job at Disney World as a medic, under a new name."[8] These are merely daydreams, of course, comfortably rejected not only because Louis genuinely loves that noisy family but also because he believes dreams to be just dreams, much needed fantasies that serve to redirect and release tension. It is a rational belief, a scientist's view of the irrational.

Louis trusts the mundane sanity that he himself exemplifies. His is a three score and ten philosophy, in which men do what they can to live happily before the inevitable injustice of death. Essentially agnostic, he has little concern with anything beyond life. Nonetheless, his inherent humanity makes him a good man under ordinary conditions. Lacking Victor's ego and imagination, he knows that science is a limited force, able sometimes to prolong life but never to return it. "Clocks run down—that's all I know," he tells his daughter Ellie, who at five is looking for assurance against the possibility of her beloved pet dying (p. 36). It is cold comfort that he offers her, but he does so "Because, as a doctor, he knew that death was, except perhaps for childbirth, the most natural thing in the world" (p. 42). He can accept this fact because all men must.

That is, he can accept this fact in theory; in reality, he finds it more difficult to take. On his first day at the school infirmary, a student dies in a bloody mishap, deeply disturbing Louis and everyone else around. That night the doctor dreams (at least, he refuses to call the experience anything but a dream) that the dead boy has come to warn him against approaching destruction, something to do with the local pet cemetery that had earlier worried Ellie. Despite physical evidence proving that the incident involved if not an actual ghost at least some physical danger, Louis labels the occurrence a nightmare caused by stress. He concentrates hard on rationalizing it away.

The next nightmare is much harder to reason past. It should be impossible to reason out for it concerns impossibility. When Church, Ellie's cat, is killed on the highway, the little girl, her mother, and her baby brother are out of town; but Dr. Creed is home. Knowing he cannot heal a corpse any more than he will be able to prevent his daughter's tears, Louis resigns himself to burying Church in that old "pet sematary." Instead, at the behest of his very old and often wise neighbor, Jud Crandall, he carries the cat to the wilds beyond the sematary, to an ancient Indian burial ground. (Thus, *sematary* is not just a childish misspelling of *cemetery*; it is an indication that this particular graveyard is connected to something other than the ordinary resting place.) Louis inters the animal deep in the Indian ground, where it is, apparently, resurrected from the grave. It comes home, seemingly a free gift of some god; soon enough, though, the astonished doctor realizes a price has been paid. Smelling of corruption, stumbling with clumsiness, the cat has become a beast, not just a hunter but a torturer and a devourer of small things. Like the Creature assembled out of death, Church is now unnatural, unfit for life.

And his owner has participated in the change. As he takes the cat with its broken neck up a deadfall and through a swamp toward the magic Micmac ground, Louis remembers what the dream ghost told him:

> Don't go beyond, no matter how much you feel you need to, Doctor. The barrier was not made to be broken.
>
> But now, tonight, that dream or warning or whatever it had been seemed years rather than months distant. Louis felt fine and fey and alive, ready to cope with anything, and yet full of wonder. It occurred to him that *this* was very much like a dream. (pp. 107-108)

Hours later, back in his own bed where he lies exhausted from the night journey, he hears the ghost approach and thinks, "'Let me alone...what's done is done and what's dead is dead'—and the steps faded away" (p. 124). The spectre of caution never returns.

Even without his guardian spirit, however, Louis can still reason. On considering the cat his children will no longer be able to love, he reaches all the right conclusions:

Church had been dead, that was one thing; he was alive now and that was another; there was something fundamentally different, fundamentally *wrong* about him, and that was a third. Something had happened. Jud had repaid what he saw as a favor...but the medicine available at the Micmac burying ground was perhaps not such good medicine, and Louis now saw something in Jud's eyes that told him the old man knew it. (p. 139)

Even now, with his hands soiled by digging beyond the barrier, Louis understands when Jud, troubled by his part in Church's resurrection, explains that the burial ground is tainted, given over by the Indians to a Wendigo, a malevolent demon of the wilds. Those who use such an evil spirit cannot often free themselves of it. Jud used it as a boy to revive his dog; now Louis has trafficked with it as a man.

A more superstitious man would run. Perhaps a wiser man would, too. Louis is neither superstitious nor wise, merely rational. Rationality, of course, has nothing to do with the pet sematary, nothing whatsoever to do with the spirit on its other side. A 20th-century man, Louis with his reliance on reasoned-out reality is an exceptionally easy mark for the Wendigo. His very rationality betrays him, for when his two-year old son Gage, his beloved only son, dies like Church run over on the highway outside his home, Louis can turn neither to science nor to religion for comfort.[9] Gage was his joy. Now the joy is gone, taken in a vicious accident (the doctor does not see until much too late the curious timing of that accident). Dreaming of his son growing to adolescence, dating pretty girls, winning an Olympic swim meet, Louis cannot keep the fact of Gage's death from entering the dream. The bitter nature of that fact separates him from both his family and his calling. Everyone expects him to be a healer, to help his wife Rachel and their surviving child. He cannot. He lets Rachel "cry beside him, uncomforted" (p. 217); he lets Ellie "swim in her grief as best she could" (p. 253). He rationalizes again, finding his thoughts "too full of his son" to have room for others (p. 253).

Now, Louis' thoughts cloud over, as he muses, "Church had by no means turned into Frankencat" (p. 226). Immediately, he knows this reflection for a lie, but the lie has let him think about the unthinkable, human resurrection. And it is not love for his broken son that holds him to the thought; it is that "In spite of everything, the idea had that deadly attraction, that sick luster, that *glamour*. Yes, that above all else— it had *glamour*" (p. 227). It is Victor Frankenstein's dream in its final stage: after creation comes renewal. Working, like Victor, in a trance,

Louis steals his baby's remains from the grave and moves them to the Micmac burial ground. Along the way, he loses his sanity, rationality, his very humanity.[10] Jud had warned him that someone else once tried to bring back a human; what actually came back was a monster. The ghost had already warned him. Church had been a warning in clammy cat flesh. Even Ellie, through some obscure precognitive shine, had tried to warn her daddy. Louis doesn't care now. He belongs to the Wendigo— and so does his son.

Little Gage Creed does come back—not as a dream of new life but as another nightmare made real. What the Wendigo does is to resurrect the corpse and infuse it with the demon's own malignity. Jud Crandall, in his last moments on earth, sees what has been done to Gage, age two when he died:

> Gage Creed came in, dressed in his burial suit. Moss was growing on the suit's shoulders and lapels. Moss had fouled his white shirt. His fine blond hair was caked with dirt. One eye had gone to the wall; it stared off into space with terrible concentration. The other was fixed on Jud.
>
> Gage was grinning at him.
>
> "Hello, Jud," Gage piped in a babyish but perfectly understandable voice. "I've come to send your rotten, stinking old soul straight to hell." (p. 345)

With a scalpel stolen from its father's bag, the Gage monster then slaughters the octogenarian Jud Crandall. Soon after, this thing with the body of a toddler murders and partially devours its mother while its father sleeps. Having dreamt that the Wendigo had "turned him into not just a cannibal but the father of cannibals" (p. 353), Louis gets up to find the massacre. Deliberately, he traps the cat and his son, rekills them, and retires to a corner just to think. Everything should be over, but the phantasm that has become Louis' reality does not end. Still entranced as he watches the body of his wife, the doctor can think of no way to heal her beyond the gruesomely obvious: he rushes Rachel's body to the wilds beyond the pet sematary. In the book's epilogue, she— it—comes back:

> A cold hand fell on Louis's shoulder. Rachel's voice was grating, full of dirt.
> "*Darling*," it said.

With that word, the novel breaks off, unconcluded.

It can have no conclusion. Dreams never do. Victor dreams of successful creation almost to his last breath, and yet he dies. Louis dreams of joyous resurrection in the very face of demonic possession, and still the carnage continues. For Stephen King as for Mary Shelley, there is always the need for caution. Man must dream; but if life, with its hard

and narrow limitations, is to be accepted for what it truly is rather than
what it should have been, the dreamer must sometimes wake up.

Notes

¹Mary Wollstonecraft Shelley, Introduction to the Third Edition, *Frankenstein
or The Modern Prometheus* (the 1818 text), ed. James Rieger (Indianapolis: Bobbs-
Merrill, 1974), p. 228. All further references to this edition are cited parenthetically.

²Douglas E. Winter, *Stephen King*, Starmont Reader's Guide 16 (Mercer Island,
WA: Starmont House, 1982), p. 105.

³Stephen King, *Danse Macabre* (New York: Everest House, 1981), p. 34.

⁴*Ibid.*, p. 65.

⁵See King's introductions to *Frankenstein/Dracula/Dr. Jekyll and Mr. Hyde* (New
York: Signet, 1978) and *Frankenstein, or The Modern Prometheus* (New York: Dodd,
Mead, 1983).

⁶King made this response in a question and answer session following an interview
with Douglas E. Winter, at The Fifth International Conference on the Fantastic in
the Arts, Boca Raton, FL, March 23, 1984.

⁷Interview with Douglas E. Winter, May 3, 1982, rpt. in *Stephen King*, p. 106.

⁸Stephen King, *Pet Sematary* (Garden City, NY: Doubleday, 1983), p. 4. All further
references to this work are cited parenthetically.

⁹According to Douglas E. Winter, "King named Ellie's cat with a purpose; in
the death of Church, he signals that the issue at the heart of *Pet Sematary* is that
of the rational being's struggle with modern death—death without God, death without
hope of salvation" (*Stephen King: The Art of Darkness* [New York: NAL, 1984],
p. 133). The NAL book is a later version of Winter's Starmont work.

¹⁰King has said of Louis, "He never ceases to be the rational man" (Interview
with Douglas E. Winter, Jan, 15, 1984, rpt. in *The Art of Darkness*, p. 134). However,
it could perhaps be said rather that Louis never ceases to be a rationalizing man,
reshaping logic in his mind to suit his—and the Wendigo's—desires.

Stephen King's *Pet Sematary*: Hawthorne's Woods Revisited

Tony Magistrale

"Is not this better," murmured he, "than what we dreamed of in the forest?"
"I know not! I know not!" she hurriedly replied.

(*The Scarlet Letter*, 236)

Stephen King's fictional allegories owe much of their formulation to, and are reminiscent of, the romance tradition in nineteenth and twentieth-century American literature. Like Poe, Melville, Hawthorne, and Flannery O'Connor, King often places his protagonists in situations where they encounter the reality of evil, and from this encounter they must make choices which will influence the remainder of their lives. How his characters react to the loss of innocence is a central theme in King's work; their ability to survive is dependent upon what they learn from the fall from grace.

As is so often the case in Hawthorne's canon, the awareness of sin forces King's characters to proceed in one of two possible directions. The first is toward moral regeneration, a spirit of renewed commitment to other human beings that is born from an acceptance of the devil's thesis as postulated in "Young Goodman Brown," that "Evil is the nature of mankind" (98), and that the failure to acknowledge either the existence of evil or its nexus to mankind results in spiritual death. On the other hand, the discovery of sin can frequently be overwhelming; it does not always lead to a higher state of moral consciousness. In Hawthorne and King, the encounter with evil is often portrayed as an experience that leads to isolation and self-destruction. Characters in their fictions commit their worst transgressions in refusing to recognize the evil in themselves, and in failing to exert a greater measure of self-discipline.

Dr. Louis Creed, the protagonist in Stephen King's 1983 novel *Pet Sematary*, shares much in common with the darkest characters in Hawthorne. Creed is similar to the impassioned, but misguided idealists who populate Hawthorne's stories; he resembles Aylmer, Rappaccini,

126

Chillingworth, Goodman Brown and Hollingsworth who also fail to recognize the inviolable distinction separating human idealism from the limitations of reality. Like these characters in Hawthorne, Creed violates standards for personal moral conduct and brings about his own destruction.

Early in the novel we learn of Doctor Creed's perspective on death. In response to his daughter's anger over the prospect of someday losing her cat to the mysterious force that has populated the Pet Sematary, Creed responds that "'Clocks run down—that's all I know. There are no guarantees, babe' " (36). Creed's controlled attitude toward death infuriates both his daughter and wife. They see nothing "natural" in the abrupt negation of life. But more important, the novel will also reveal that Creed himself does not believe that death "'is the most natural thing in the w[orld]' " (41). His disciplined attitude is merely a veneer that is shattered when his own child is killed. When confronted with the reality of his child's death, Creed displays his inherent inability to maintain a rational perspective towards immortality. After Louis loses his only son, he seeks to repudiate death's dominion over the human world by availing himself of the resuscitative energies residing within an Indian burial ground located in the woods several miles behind his home.

In the nineteenth century, Emerson and the transcendentalists assured their audience that nature represented a vehicle to true self-knowledge. King and Hawthorne certainly concur with this premise, although the self disclosed by Thoreau in the pines at Walden pond is vastly different than what Louis Creed and Goodman Brown uncover in the wilderness behind their respective communities. Instead of a mirror to the self's purity and limitless potentiality that the transcendentalists associated with New England nature, the woods of Hawthorne and King are a reflection of the self's essential darkness and the human affinity to sin.

The journey into the wilderness in Hawthorne's fiction is always fraught with danger. Within the New England pines of Hawthorne's symbolic landscapes we find the powerful rhythms of primordial and uncontrollable forces. Hawthorne's Puritan ancestors fully comprehended that within the uncut trees surrounding their early enclaves lurked elements that were seldom benevolently disposed toward human welfare. In the woods, one could easily lose direction, encounter hostile Indians and animals, or worse yet, be forced into an immediate struggle with Satan's legions. As Heinrich Zimmer explains in *The King and the Corpse*,

The forest has always been a place of initiation for there the demonic presences, the ancestral spirits, and the forces of nature reveal themselves. The forest is the antithesis of house and heart, village and field boundary, where the household gods hold sway and where human laws and customs prevail. It holds the dark forbidden things—secrets, terrors, which threaten the protected life of the ordered world of common day. (69)

The Scarlet Letter, "Roger Malvin's Burial," "Young Goodman Brown" and "Ethan Brand" all mirror the Puritan influence on Hawthorne's work. When the protagonist in each of these tales ventures forth into the forest, he returns to his respective village and family in a transformed state. Within the New World forest, Hawthorne imagined a bifurcated vision: the danger of Faustian temptation as well as the possibility for rebirth and transcendence.

Dimmesdale and Reuben Bourne are made to face the realities of their own self-deceptions in the woods; the journey into the dark pines becomes a metaphor for a journey into the self. Separated from the hypocritical pressures of civilized life, Dimmesdale and Bourne acknowledge the true depravity of their natures; from this profound recognition of the evil within themselves, each man emerges from the woods chastened, his life dramatically altered.

Like Dimmesdale, Reuben Bourne is living a lie; his failure to provide Roger Malvin with a Christian burial, coupled with his unwillingness to tell Dorcas the truth about her father's abandonment in the woods, create "a moody and misanthropic man...feeling few regrets and disdaining to acknowledge any" (19). In order to confront his sins and gain forgiveness for them, Bourne must re-enter the woods and acknowledge his repressed guilt: "...in the calmest and clearest moods of his mind, he was conscious that he had a deep vow unredeemed, and that an unburied corpse was calling to him out of the wilderness" (17). The wilderness serves Bourne in a psychoanalytic capacity; by forcing him into contact with that part of himself that he has willfully denied, Reuben's journey takes him deeper into the woods—and by symbolic extension, deeper into himself: "[he] strayed onward rather like a sleepwalker than a hunter" (22). Hawthorne's use of a somnambulistic analogy is important here, as it highlights the function of the woods as a representational arena for the unconscious self, the place where Bourne confronts his darkest impulses, and where civilized hypocrisies are finally stripped clean. As Reginald Cook argues in "The Forest of Goodman Brown's Night: A Reading of Hawthorne's 'Young Goodman Brown,' " Hawthorne's symbolic forests reveal the very turbulence of the human mind, "the form its guilt takes, the contributions of grace and election, the sense of justice, the invocation of mercy" (478).

Over the years, Bourne's sins have corroded his soul: "[his] insulated emotions had gradually made a selfish man, and he could no longer love deeply except where he saw or imagined some reflection or likeness of his own mind" (19). Since Bourne recognizes in his young son Cyrus, "what he himself had been in other days" (19), his child's murder serves as a symbolic death of Bourne himself—the destruction of that part of his psyche, long sustained by a posture of deceptive innocence, which has produced his guilt and anxiety. Bourne's purification is achieved at the expense of his son's life in order to appease "a voice audible only to himself, commanding him to go forth and redeem his vow" (18). In satisfying this primitive "voice" that Reuben hears deep in the woods, his son's blood opens the way to the civilized virtues of exculpation, reconciliation, and a renewal of his Christian faith.

Young Goodman Brown and Ethan Brand are also profoundly changed by their experience in the woods, but for these characters the struggle against the evil they discover there is not positively resolved. Neither Brown nor Brand is spiritually transformed by the insights they gain in the forest; in fact, unlike Dimmesdale or Bourne, Brown and Brand forfeit the opportunity for personal salvation when they reject their bond with the community of sin openly acknowledged in the woods.

Louis Creed's journey into the trees behind his house shares more in common with the negative voyages in "Young Goodman Brown" and "Ethan Brand" than with the redemptive encounters portrayed in "Roger Malvin's Burial" and *The Scarlet Letter*. King's Wendigo, the wrathful Indian spirit that animates the unholy Micmac burial ground beyond the Pet Sematary and deadfall, exploits human weakness and vulnerability; it thrives on the doctor's inability to discipline his curiosity and to recognize the distinction between saving lives and playing god. As is the situation in Hawthorne's tales, the woods in King's novel reveal man's penchant for evil, his innate depravity; but unlike the forests of "Young Goodman Brown" or *The Scarlet Letter*, which offer at least the possibility for spiritual advancement concurrent with an acceptance of personal sin, the wild god of King's wilderness makes no such compromises with Louis Creed. Hawthorne's natural landscapes appear to be animated by subtle forces that ultimately invite his protagonists into a confrontation with ethical codes and principles. As "Roger Malvin's Burial" illustrates, the trek into the woods often serves as an unsentimental journey toward moral instruction. In contrast, King's Wendigo is thoroughly amoral: it manipulates human trust through the promised miracle of resurrection—only to deliver a grotesque version of itself.

Goodman Brown and Ethan Brand discover that the forest is much darker and more ominous than they originally anticipated, and Louis Creed eventually gains a similar insight. Each time the doctor ventures into the Indian cemetery, he, like Brown and Brand, experiences a greater level of human estrangement. The encounter with evil narrows each of these men into a position where they become less sensitive to the "magnetic chain of humanity" (285) and more involved with themselves and their own personal quests. Brown's wandering into the woods reveals a progressively deepening awareness of the pervasiveness of evil. The revelation that his perspective on the nature of his community, clergy, ancestors, and even his wife has been naive and inaccurate, pushes Brown from a state of innocence to one of cynical despair. Unable to accept the reality of evil in either humankind or himself, Brown "shrank from the bosom of Faith; and at morning or eventide, when the family knelt down at prayer, he scowled and muttered to himself, and gazed sternly at his wife, and turned away" (100).

As Brown's encounter with evil produces a retreat into himself, Louis Creed's deepening involvement with the dark powers of the Wendigo likewise alienates the doctor from his own family and community. Indeed, Creed's obsession with bringing his son back to life is indulged at the expense of his other, nearly catatonic child and desolate wife: "There had been times in the dark watches of the night when she [his wife] had longed to hate Louis for the grief he had fathered inside her, and for not giving her the comfort she needed... " (324).   Contemplating a second trip to the burial ground to bring about his son's resurrection, Louis Creed's isolation finds a parallel in Goodman Brown's "dying hour [of] gloom" (100) and Ethan Brand's break from "the universal throb...of brother man" (285). That feeling of coldness still held; he felt totally unplugged from his people, the places that had become so familiar to him, even his work....Madness was all around him, softly fluttering as the wings of night-hunting owls with great golden eyes: he was heading into madness. (278)

In the fictions of Hawthorne and King there are definite realms of experience that highlight man's limitations, his inability to grasp, much less to manipulate, the mysteries found in nature and deep within the human heart. Hawthorne's idealists engage actions that violate moral barriers—whether in the form of perverse scientific quests (as in "The Birthmark" and "Rappaccini's Daughter") or through personal intrusions into the secrets of another human being (as in the actions of Chillingworth and Ethan Brand). Terence Martin observes in "The Method of Hawthorne's Tales," that "the cancer of obsession threatens any Hawthorne character—scientist, man of religion, artist—who prefers an idea to a human being" (17). Louis Creed's self-corruption occurs as a result of a similar transgression: he consciously chooses to liberate the malevolent energies residing in the Micmac burial ground because he wishes control over the ability to regulate life and sustain existence.

Like Hawthorne's doctors, Aylmer and Rappaccini, Creed sacrifices the people who are dearest to him because of his obsession with an idea: the challenge of altering the immutable laws of nature. While it is possible to argue persuasively that Creed is initially drawn to the Micmac burial site because of an altruistic love for his daughter and the desire to spare her the pain of grief over a lost cat, by the conclusion of the novel altruism is no longer the doctor's primary motivation. Creed's compulsion to deliver the bodies of his son and wife to the cemetery is not adequately explained as a consequence of his guilt and grief. Rather, he is more interested in continuing his misguided experiment under the irrational premise that eventually he will discover a way to dominate death.

At various points throughout the book Creed appears to be keeping an unconscious personal record against death. Each time his medical skills aid in saving a human life, Creed whispers to himself, " 'won one today, Louis' " (161). Creed's game against the reaper continues even as the stakes grow ever larger. Although he has listened to repeated warnings about the treacherous nature of the place and has even witnessed first hand the monstrous consequences of his son's resurrection, the doctor remains convinced of his ability to manipulate the powers residing in the burial ground. As a result of his refusal to accept the workings of Fate, he is transformed into an extension of the amoral Wendigo. Like the insistent Aylmer in Hawthorne's tale "The Birthmark," who willingly squanders his beautiful wife for the sake of testing a scientific theory, Creed sacrifices himself and those around him in his obsession to unlock the mystery that will yield the secret of immortality: "'I waited too long with Gage,' Louis said. 'Something got into him because I waited too long. But it will be different with Rachel, Steve. I know it will' " (370).

In spite of the mechanistic world-view maintained in most gothic fiction, the characters in King and Hawthorne still possess a persuasive element of free will. The majority of their protagonists are like Louis Creed: they choose their own course of action. It is an act of Ethan Brand's own volition that leads him to pursue the Unpardonable Sin, just as Goodman Brown's gloom is a result of his choice to emphasize only the "despair" and none of the "triumph" voiced by Satan's congregation in their communal awareness of evil (98). As Robert Deamer points out in "Hawthorne's Dream in the Forest," "[Brown] did not *have* to journey into the forest and to indulge in doubts of Faith or in visions of orgiastic evil. Faced with the choice of loving his wife or believing in his religion, he chose, disastrously for him, to do the latter" (334).

While it may be true that the Micmac burial ground possesses, as Crandall asserts, " 'a power...and it's coming around to full again' " (246),   Creed freely elects to avail himself of its insidious magic. He essentially acknowledges his terrible freedom moments before he begins his son's disinterment: "his heart told him quietly and absolutely that he couldn't come back tomorrow. If he didn't do it tonight, he could never do it. He would never be able to screw himself up to this crazy pitch again....This was the moment, the only time for it he was ever going to have" (297). Moreover, Creed makes his decision to re-enter the enchanted woods in a flagrant rejection of Victor Pascow's prophetic warning. Pascow's recent death provides immediate insight into the malevolence which resides in the Indian burial ground, and he tries in vain to share this vision with Creed: " 'The door must not be opened.... The barrier was not meant to be broken. Remember this: there is more power here than you know. *It* is old and always restless.... Your destruction and the destruction of all you love is very near, Doctor' " (70).

In light of Creed's election to disregard Pascow's message, it is interesting that Jud Crandall, who is responsible for introducing the doctor to the transformational properties inherent in the Micmac soil, is soon placed in a position to employ its life-giving powers. After learning that Norma, Jud's beloved wife, has died suddenly, Creed's first thought is of "Jud pulling Norma's corpse on a pagan litter through the woods. Toward the Micmac burial ground beyond the Pet Sematary" (173). But unlike Creed, Jud is capable of exercising a greater measure of self-control; he rejects the temptation to resurrect Norma. His memory of Timmy Baterman remains a vivid illustration of the Wendigo's devastating influence over human interments, and this recollection serves as a sufficient deterrent to keep Jud from further experimentation. Not only is Crandall capable of restraining the selfish impulse to play God by summoning Norma back to life, but he also supplies Creed, after the latter loses his son, with advice that echoes Pascow's warning: "'You know why I'm here,' Jud said. 'You're thinking about things that are not to be thought of, Louis. Worse still, I fear you're considering them' " (230).

Throughout Hawthorne's fiction, his protagonists are offered sage counsel and guidance during the course of their moral struggles. In "My Kinsman, Major Molineux" a friendly stranger encourages Robin to seek alternatives to the patronage of his kinsman or a return ticket home. Mary Goffe reminds Richard Digby of his relationship to other human beings and tries to lure him away from his isolation in "The Man of Adamant." Similarly, Hester Prynne is Dimmesdale's model of endurance and courage in *The Scarlet Letter*. And in "The Birthmark" Aminadab, Aylmer's laboratory assistant, immediately identifies the danger inherent in his employer's quest to remove Georgiana's facial flaw, muttering " 'If she were my wife, I'd never part with that birthmark' " (209). Each of these characters parallels Jud Crandall's role in *Pet Sematary*: they are presented as sensible counterpoints to the encroaching madness of the central protagonists. Like Jud, they embody the human requisite to recognize and exercise a measure of control over the self's most debased and indulgent urges. Moreover, they offer unsentimental alternatives to the main character's choice of action, reminding him of obligations that challenge the limitations of egotism. If their examples and/or advice is emulated, the protagonist usually endures; if rebuffed, self-destruction is the inevitable consequence.

In *Pet Sematary* Stephen King captures the native speech patterns, the elements of life in a cold climate, and the specificity of place that set his readers firmly in a rural Maine world. King is a regionalist for many of the same reasons that Hawthorne chose to write about Massachusetts: each author understands that the universal themes of great literature—human sin, fear, and endurance—can only be rendered truthfully within settings and by personalities an artist has come to know on a first-hand basis. Much as Hawthorne relied on Puritan New England as a setting to describe the foibles and sins that are the inheritance of humanity, King views Maine as a deliberate backdrop for his own allegories, enabling him to utilize specific elements from that culture in his portrayal of the moral conflicts common to us all.

The events which transpire in the woods behind the Pet Sematary are reminiscent of the narrative pattern which occurs in Hawthorne's fiction. An individual loses his innocence in the encounter with tragic circumstances and is faced with the struggle to redefine himself morally. In portraying the negative results of this struggle, both writers suggest that there are certain mysteries man must simply learn to accept, certain secrets he has no business attempting to discover, and certain ethical barriers that he only transcends at the expense of his soul. Hawthorne's tales and King's novel achieve their power in demonstrating that one's humanity is dreadfully easy to lose, and what we abandon ourselves to possess, we necessarily become. The romantic poet William Blake may have felt perfect harmony residing in "the lineaments of gratified desire," but for King and Hawthorne the inevitable end of such self-absorption is the madness of Louis Creed circling back through the woods for another trip to the Micmac burial grounds or the devastation of Ethan Brand's marbled heart.

Works Cited

Cook, Reginald. "The Forest of Young Goodman Brown's Night: A Reading of Hawthorne's 'Young Goodman Brown.'" *New England Quarterly* 43 (1970), 473-481.

Deamer, Robert Glen. "Hawthorne's Dream in the Forest." *Western American Literature* 13:4 (1979), 327-340.

Hawthorne, Nathaniel. *The Celestial Railroad and Other Stories.* New York: New American Library, 1963.

Hawthorne, Nathaniel. *The Scarlet Letter.* New York: New American Library, 1959.

King, Stephen. *Pet Sematary.* New York: Doubleday, 1983.

Martin, Terence. "The Method of Hawthorne's Tales" in *Nathaniel Hawthorne: A Collection of Criticism.* Ed. J. Donald Crowley. New York: McGraw-Hill, 1975.

Zimmer, Heinrich. *The King and the Corpse.* New Jersey: Princeton University Press, 1957.

"Oz the Gweat and Tewwible" and "The Other Side": The Theme of Death in *Pet Sematary* and *Jitterbug Perfume*

Natalie Schroeder

In his Forward to *Night Shift*, Stephen King attributes the popularity of horror fiction to man's fascination with and fear of death:

> Fear makes us blind, and we touch each fear with the avid curiosity of self-interest, trying to make a whole out of a hundred parts,...
>
> We sense the shape. Children grasp it easily, forget it, and relearn it as adults. The shape is there, and most of us come to realize what it is sooner or later. All our fears add up to one great fear, all our fears are part of that great fear—an arm, a leg, a finger, an ear. We're afraid of the body under the sheet. It's our body. And the great appeal of horror fiction through the ages is that it serves as a rehearsal for our own deaths. (xvi)

The treatment of death in best-sellers, of course, varies: some writers use death to manipulate the plot and others to exploit readers' emotions. Still others, like Stephen King and Tom Robbins, treat death thematically. Novels like *Pet Sematary* and *Jitterbug Perfume* are escape fiction, but they also help readers explore their own fears of what Hamlet calls "The undiscovered country, from whose bourn / No traveler returns..." (III.i, 79-80).

Both King and Robbins have created characters who fear or resent death, and both treat man's concern for an afterlife. In fact, in each novel at least one character defies Hamlet and returns from the "undiscovered country." The basic subject of the two novels is the same, and so is their ultimate message: we must work to overcome our fears of death, for dying is a natural process which no one can defeat. Although King and Robbins agree that man may fight death only within natural limits, finally their attitudes toward death differ. In perhaps the most shocking horror novel he has yet written, King reveals his own "great fear" of death. In his comic fantasy, Robbins tends to blunt death's sting and trivialize its importance to life.

At the beginning of *Pet Sematary*, Louis Creed, a lapsed Methodist, is a rational doctor who views death as the end of all things, but rather than fear death, he accepts it as a part of life. Indeed, like childbirth, to him it is the most "natural thing in the world" (56). His wife's attitude and experience are different. As an eight-year-old child she alone witnessed the death of her monstrous sister. Now death terrifies Rachel, and this terror manifests itself in her violent fury when Louis tries to discuss death rationally with her. After a visit to the Pet Sematary, their five-year-old daughter Ellie also begins to fear death. The graves of the dead animals make her worry that Church, her cat will die, and if a cat can die, it "could happen to her mother, her father, her baby brother. To herself. Death was a vague idea; the Pet Sematary was real" (51).

Death does come first to her cat and then to her baby brother Gage, but each death is followed by a resurrection. After a truck mangles Church, Louis blindly follows Jud Crandall, his best friend and second father, and buries the cat in the Micmac burial ground. Although Louis does not intentionally resurrect Church, he learns that nevertheless he must bear the responsibility for his actions. Church, returned from the dead is loathsome to Louis, and because King fills his prose with minute realistic details, he lures the reader into a temporary suspension of disbelief in the supernatural:

> There was dried blood caked on Church's muzzle, and caught in his long whiskers were two tiny shreds of green plastic. Bits of Hefty Bag....
> He let Church into the house, got his blue dish, and opened a tuna-and-liver cat dinner. As he spooned the gray-brown mess out of the can, Church purred unevenly and rubbed back and forth along Louis's ankles. The feel of the cat caused Louis to break out in gooseflesh, and he had to clench his teeth grimly to keep from kicking him away. His furry sides felt somehow too slick, too thick....(151)

Thus King implies the possibility of the impossible—that given the right circumstances, pets and humans can return from the dead.

Although Louis continues to find Church disgusting and eventually even demonic, the cat's resurrection gives Louis a new sort of faith. He no longer believes death is the end, but rather that man and animals "go on." "But as to what it's like," he tells Ellie, "I have no opinion. It may be that it's different for different people. It may be that you get what you believed all your life" (201).

The death of his infant son Gage, however, turns the newly-faithful Louis Creed into a blasphemous madman. The doctor who could rationally accept the violent death of Victor Pascow and later the peaceful death of Norma Crandall, and who earlier, after Gage almost choked, calmly told his wife, "honey...we're all close [to death]. All the time" (182),—that same doctor cannot accept his son's accidental death.

Extenuating circumstances contribute to his inability to cope, however. First of all Louis blames himself for not running fast enough to stop his son from running into the road. More importantly, he fears that the powers he stirred up in the Micmac burial ground may have claimed Gage's life in exchange for Church's.

King leaves the ultimate causes of Louis's behavior ambiguous. Either he is completely controlled by the supernatural powers of the burying ground, which demand a human (albeit dead) sacrifice. Or, in his overwhelming grief at the loss of his child, Louis reaches for any possible way to get his child back—even to committing what he knows is blasphemy, by playing God knowingly this time and resurrecting Gage. Throughout the grave robbing episode, Louis's rational side debates with his irrational side. He wonders if he is really controlling his own actions; why he can't remember what his son looked like; why he is ignoring Victor Pascow's and Jud Crandall's warnings; and why he is ignoring his own guilty conscience. Louis's decision at this juncture is all the more terrifying because he acts of his own free will: *"Louis,"* he tells himself as he is about to remove the body from the grave, *"I think this is it. Your last chance. You're right,"* he answers himself, *"It's my last chance and I'm damned well taking it"* (336).

In resurrecting Gage, Louis consciously disregards the wisdom in Jud Crandall's first explanation for taking Louis to the Micmac burial ground: "Maybe I did it because kids need to know that sometimes dead is better.... That's somethin your Ellie don't know, and I got a feelin that maybe she don't know because your wife don't know.... Maybe she'll learn something about what death really is, which is where the pain stops and the good memories begin. Not the end of life but the end of pain" (166, 167). With Gage gone, however, to Louis death is no longer a natural part of life, but rather an evil villain. By resurrecting Gage, he tries to defeat man's frightening enemy, personified as "Oz the Gweat and Tewwible," who is:

waiting to choke you on a marble, to smother you with a dry-cleaning bag, to sizzle you into eternity with a fast and lethal boggie of electricity—Available at Your Nearest Switchplate or Vacant Light Socket Right Now. There was death in a quarter bag of peanuts, an aspirated piece of steak, the next pack of cigarettes. He was around all the time, he monitored all the checkpoints between the mortal and the eternal.... Hi, folks, my name's Oz the Gweat and Tewwible, but you can call me Oz if you want—hell, we're old friends by now. Just stopped by to whop you with a little congestive heart failure or a cranial blood clot or something; can't stay, got to see a woman about a breach birth, then I've got a little smoke-inhalation job to do in Omaha. (375-376)

Too late—shortly before his resurrected demonic monster-son returns to kill Jud and Rachel violently and before Louis turns into a white-haired lunatic—he realizes that the battle against "Oz the Gweat and Tewwible" is a "hopeless" one (376). Louis ultimately blames himself not the burial ground for his tragedy. He realizes that his fatal flaw was his not uncommon "inability to accept" death. The burial ground fed on his grief and sanity: "It's cost you your wife," he thinks, "and it's almost surely cost you your best friend as well as your son" (395).

King indirectly shows us how to deal with death through Jud's quiet acceptance of his wife's death and, more specifically, what *not* to do through Louis's behavior. The poignant descriptions of Gage's funeral and the effects of the fatal accident on all the members of the Creed family are cathartic; furthermore the Wendingo monster and child-demon are not just ghosties and ghoulies that go bump in the night—creatures included solely for a sensational effect—they are symbolic metaphors for uncontrolled grief and its potential for self and community destruction.

In *Pet Sematary* King also affirms the notion of an afterlife not through the grotesque resurrections of Church, Gage, and Rachel, but through Victor Pascow's discorporated soul, who first warns Louis and later Ellie. Second, in the chilling conclusion of the novel, Rachel, newly arisen from her "grave" puts her cold hand on Louis's shoulder and says, *"Darling,"* in a "grating" voice, "full of dirt" (411). That gesture indicates that in one brief sentence, Jud articulates King's point: "Sometimes dead *is* better" (emphasis mine).

The tone of Tom Robbins's *Jitterbug Perfume* differs radically from King's. Robbins takes a comic stance on the topic of death and thus undercuts man's fear of it. His fanciful portrayal of the afterlife affirms the importance of a lighthearted approach to mortal existence. Robbins develops the theme of death and immortality through the comic fable of Alobar, a 1,000 year old past king of Bohemia, Kudra, his voluptuous wife, and Dr. Dannyboy Wiggs, a former flowerchild of the 60's.

Alobar and Kudra's battles with death differ from Louis Creed's. They run from their own deaths and seek an immortality by gaining "some influence over the unknown tribunal that sentences us to die against our wishes. A reform of that law that decrees death a certain consequence of birth" (115-116). In the abandoned Caves of the Bandaloops, they learn that "physical immortality is not an end result, a condition to be arrived at in the future, but an ongoing discipline, an attitude, a way of life to be practiced in the present, day by day" (151). By eating properly, taking long hot baths, enjoying regular sexual activity, breathing properly, and thinking positively, they stop aging.

Like Louis Creed, but in their own way, they play God. Also like Louis, they occasionally worry that they are being blasphemous. Kudra, for example, feels that in "defying death, she was doing something wrong and would be made to pay for it in some prolonged and unspeakably excruciating way" (158). Alobar worries that he may be "inviting a revenge worse than simple annihilation" (159). Kudra's visit to "The Other Side," however, indicates that rather than an invitation to damnation, their lifestyle assures them of permanent immortality.

Alobar's situation comes somewhat closer to Louis Creed's when Kudra dematerializes. Grief stricken, Alobar does not know if Kudra is dead or if she can return. "Death," he says, "can ruin a man's life even though he go on breathing" (219). But unlike Louis, Alobar curtails his mourning so that his life won't "become a deathly imitation through depression and sorrow" (219). He vows to obey the mysterious message (presumably from "The Other Side") to "lighten up" and strives always to keep a sense of play in his mind. He continues in this fashion for centuries until, thrown in prison and unable to practice his immortality exercises, he begins to age.

Dr. Dannyboy Wiggs also defies death, and in between comically graphic lovemaking scenes, he tells Priscilla Partido, the "genius waitress," about his own quest for immortality. He first felt the specter of death when he was in prison, and his description of death as an enemy closely resembles Louis's personification of death as Oz:

the fact of our impending death is always there, just behind the draperies, or, more accurately, inside our sock, like a burr that we can never quite extract. . . . [T]he specter is there, night and day, day in and day out, coloring with its chalk of gray almost everything we do. And a lot of what we do is done, subconsciously, indirectly, to avoid the thought of death, or to make ourselves so unexpendable through our accomplishments that death will hesitate to take us, or, when the scimitar finally falls, to insure that we "live on" in the memory of the lucky ones still kicking. (281-282)

Because Wiggs concluded that the fear of death trivializes life and that death robs life of meaning, he set out to battle it in yet another way— through study. But it was from his cellmate, "Al Barr," now a 1,000 year-old janitor, that he learned how to fight death effectively. After he was freed from prison, Wiggs established the Last Laugh Foundation, an immortality clinic, because (in his words) we have "to evolve beyond our death consciousness if we expect to claim our divine right to life everlastin'. If we expect to be i-n-g instead of e-d" (298). However only one resident immortalist stays there: Professor Morgenstern, who dances a new kind of jitterbug called the Bandaloop, what we ultimately learn is still another way to achieve longevity.

Despite his active bid for an immortality like Alobar's, Morgenstern is murdered because of man's death consciousness. The mob outside the Last Laugh Foundation breaks in, and when they see no evidence of active scientific experiments to prevent death nor any apparent clues to immortality, they panic and bash in the skulls of Morgenstern and Huxley Anne (Wiggs's daughter). While King graphically describes several horrifying deaths, Robbins maintains a comic ironic tone, even when reporting Morgenstern's violent end: "like a fertilized condor egg filled with blood and promise, the bald head of Dr. Morgenstern split open. He died instantly" (340). And Huxley Anne's miraculous recovery appears to be another resurrection, but without any King-like horrors and with typically comic causes. There are no odors among the dead because smell evokes memories that would connect the dead to life; Huxley Anne survives either because of the open bottle of White Shoulders placed beside her bed, or because the soul of a light-hearted dead man, Bingo Pajama, is reincarnated in her body. When she awakens from her month-long coma, Huxley Anne explains that our energy comes from the fact that in life our souls constantly leave our bodies. "When you die," she says, "your soul *stops* leaving your body" (343).

Robbins presents his final message about life, death, and immortality in Kudra's description of her visit to "The Other Side." After dematerializing, she finds herself in a covered wharf, an enormous building "extending for two hundred yards or more beyond the shore of some dark sea" (379). The building teems with dead "*travelers who "have left their bodies behind and are walking about in mental projections, in their ideas of their earthly bodies*" (380). They all wait in lines to go to the Weighing Room, where their hearts are cut out and weighed on brass scales. If the heart is heavier than a feather, they are sent away on a ship which sails swiftly to energy realms. Only the few dead with hearts as light as feathers are granted immortality. These immortals are free to embark on a sea voyage, to return to earth, or to inhabit some different world. Those whose hearts come close to being light enough board a decorated barge on which people are eating, drinking, and partying. One side of the barge has the name Hell painted on it, the other side, Heaven. Ultimately Kudra is bored because such death is "*as orderly as life is disorderly*" (383). She leaves "The Other Side" through a door marked neither exit nor entrance, but "lighten up" in Alobar's native Slavo-Nordic language—yet another resurrection.

Although Robbins treats both parental and conjugal love fancifully and whimsically, both Dannyboy Wiggs and Alobar voice attitudes toward death that recall Louis Creed's. Had Huxley Anne not recovered, for example, Wiggs would have abandoned his pursuit of immortality and killed himself just on the chance that he could be with her. And Alobar finally decides that life without Kudra has become meaningless; thus he makes plans to dematerialize or, if necessary, to die. The two resurrections in *Jitterbug Perfume* save the protagonists from despair and self-destruction, but they are both a *deus ex machina*.

Like King, Robbins finally concedes that despite all our attempts to evade it, death is inevitable—a natural process of life that must be accepted as such, terrifying or boring as it might be. Only by overcoming our fear of death can we "lighten up," that is, enjoy life and thus achieve the immortality that enjoyment itself affords. To put it in Robbins's words: "To physically overcome death—is that not the goal?—we must think unthinkable thoughts and ask unanswerable questions. Yet we must not lose ourselves in abstract vapors of philosophy. Death has his concrete allies, we must enlist ours. Never underestimate how much assistance, how much satisfaction, how much comfort, how much soul and transcendence there might be in a well-made taco and a cold bottle of beer" (373).

By Robbins's terms, Louis Creed enlists the wrong allies, and his inability to accept death consequently results in tragedy. Robbins's protagonists, Alobar, Kudra, and Wiggs, on the other hand, learn to overcome their fears of death so that they enjoy a satisfying—almost triumphant—experience of life. Like the beet, which appears on practically every page of *Jitterbug Perfume*, Robbins says, we must "hold on to [our] divine blush, [our] innate rosy magic, or end up brown. Once [we're] brown, [we'll] find that [we're] blue. As blue as indigo. And...that means: Indigo./ Indigoing./ Indigone." (387-388)

Both *Pet Sematary* and *Jitterbug Perfume* afford readers a temporary escape from the imminent presence of death. Stephen King regales his readers with minute descriptive details, translating the horrifying supernatural events into a cathartic preview of our own forthcoming battles with death. Tom Robbins, on the other hand, chooses not to confront human fears and emotions realistically. Instead he transmutes them into something else: a humorously fantastic tale, replete with philosophical theories, pornographic scenes, and outrageous puns.

Works Cited

King, Stephen. "Forward," *Night Shift*. New York: Signet, 1976.

_____. *Pet Sematary*. New York: Signet, 1983.

Robbins, Tom. *Jitterbug Perfume*. New York & Toronto: Bantam Books, 1984.

Contributors

Linda Badley teaches courses in English and popular culture at Middle Tennessee State University. She has published articles on contemporary metafiction, fantasy, and horror. She is working on a book, *The Medium is the Monster: Mass Culture and Contemporary Horror.*

Ray B. Browne is Editor of the *Journal of Popular Culture* and *Journal of American Culture,* and author and editor of 35 books, the latest of which are *Heroes and Humanities: Detective Fiction and Culture* and *The Spirit of Australia: The Crime Fiction of Arthur W. Upfield.*

James Egan is a Professor of English at The University of Akron. His popular culture interests include fantasy and science fiction and Gothic literature. He has published essays on H.P. Lovecraft and Joyce Carol Oates as well as several on Stephen King.

Bernard J. Gallagher teaches at Central Methodist College. He is currently working on an essay entitled, "Breaking Up Isn't Hard to Do: Psychic Disintegration in Christopher Lasch's *The Culture of Narcissism* and Stephen King's *It.*"

Leonard G. Heldreth is acting chair of the English Department at Northern Michigan University where he also teaches courses in literature, film, and composition and does weekly film reviews for WNMU-FM. Current projects include editing a collection, *"The Blood is the Life": Vampires in Literature,* and writing *The Reader's Guide to Fred Saberhagen.*

James E. Hicks, a graduate student in English at the University of Denver, has only recently given up watching late night horror movies on television. While he relishes the existential dilemma of werewolves or vampires, he has also authored articles on *Piers Plowman,* Chaucer, and Ring Lardner.

Gary C. Hoppenstand is the author of *In Search of the Paper Tiger: A Sociological Perspective of Myth, Formula and the Mystery Genre in the Entertainment Print Mass Medium, The Dime Novel Detective Book* and other books.

Vernon Hyles is a Professor of English at the University of Missouri in Columbia.

Tony Magistrale has written extensively on Stephen King and other American writers. He is the author of *Landscape of Fear: Stephen King's American Gothic* (The Popular Press) and editor of *The Shining Reader,* a collection of critical essays on *The Shining* (Starmont House).

Tom Newhouse teaches at State University College at Buffalo. He writes about popular culture and modern literature. He is a frequent contributor to the Popular Press, and is currently at work on a book about subcultures in the post-war American novel.

Mary Ferguson Pharr is an Assistant Professor of English at Florida Southern College. She received her B.A. from Eckerd College and her M.A. and Ph.D. from Vanderbilt University.

Garyn G. Roberts is an Assistant Professor at Michigan State University: He has recently edited *A Cent A Story!* and *The Night Nemesis.*

Natalie Schroeder is an Assistant Professor of English at the University of Mississippi where she teaches courses in Victorian literature and popular fiction. She has published articles on Regina Maria Roche, Charles Dickens, Walter Pater, Wilkie Collins, and W.H. Ainsworth.

Samuel Schuman is Vice President for Academic Affairs and Academic Dean at Guilford College, Greensboro, North Carolina. He is the author of books on Jacobean dramatists John Webster and Cyril Tourneur, and on Vladimir Nabokov. As Director of the Honors Program and Associate Professor of English at the University of Maine at Orono, he worked with Stephen King.

Carol A. Senf is an Assistant Professor at the Georgia Institute of Technology. She has always been interested in ghosts, goblins, vampires, and other "things that go bump in the night." She has written short pieces on both Victorian fiction and popular literature, and her book, *The Vampire in Nineteenth-Century English Fiction*, will be published this year by Popular Press.